T0288368

# RICHMOND
## Now & Then

AN ANECDOTAL HISTORY

Nick Fonda

# RICHMOND
## Now & Then

AN ANECDOTAL HISTORY

Baraka
Books

Montréal

© Baraka Books

ISBN 978-1-77186-128-1 pbk; 978-1-77186-131-1 epub; 978-1-77186-132-8 pdf; 978-1-77186-133-5 mobi/pocket

Cover photo by Nick Fonda
Book Design and Cover by Folio infographie
Editing by Barbara Rudnicka
Proofreading by Karine Fonda
Back cover drawing by Denis Palmer

Legal Deposit, 4th quarter 2017
Bibliothèque et Archives nationales du Québec
Library and Archives Canada

Published by Baraka Books of Montreal
6977, rue Lacroix
Montréal, Québec H4E 2V4
Telephone: 514 808-8504
info@barakabooks.com

Printed and bound in Quebec

Trade Distribution & Returns
Canada and the United States
Independent Publishers Group
1-800-888-4741 (IPG1);
orders@ipgbook.com

We acknowledge the support from the Société de développement des entreprises culturelles (SODEC) and the Government of Quebec tax credit for book publishing administered by SODEC.

Funded by the Government of Canada
Financé par le gouvernement du Canada | Canadä

# Contents

Part 3

## FROM RIVER TO RAIL, MID-CENTURY
## TO THE GREAT WAR

Part 4

## THE TWENTIETH CENTURY

Part 5

## TWENTY-FIRST-CENTURY ECHOES

Part 6

## FACING THE FUTURE

HALF A CENTURY AGO, the Richmond County Historical Society published a two-volume set entitled, *The Tread of Pioneers, Annals of Richmond County.* Volume 1 was published in 1966 and Volume 2 in 1968, the dates serving as bookends for Canada's centennial celebrations in 1967. It was a time of hope and optimism across the country, and a century of Confederation served to bring history more clearly into the collective consciousness. In Quebec, of course, Confederation wasn't necessarily something to celebrate. Quebec wasn't looking back so much as it was looking ahead at the new horizons being created by the Quiet Revolution.

Richmond, at the time, was still markedly English in character even if the demographic shift towards a French-speaking majority was clearly evident if not yet a *fait accompli.*

The Richmond County Historical Society had only recently been formed in 1962, on an initiative led by several of the local Women's Institutes and, in particular, Alice Dresser. The founding president of the RCHS was a brisk, energetic, committed and forceful personality. Her passing in 1965 served to spur on the writing of *The Annals*; her friends and colleagues penned their essays and reminiscences with Dresser as much in mind as the dawning of Canada's second century.

Just as 1967 was a celebratory year for Canadians, so too was 2017, the country's sesquicentennial. It was a less noteworthy anniversary for the small town nestled on the St. Francis River in Quebec's Eastern Townships; incorporated as a town in 1882, Richmond was one hundred and thirty-five years old in 2017. This was not on a par with Quebec City's four hundredth anniversary in 2008, nor with Montreal's three hundred and seventy-fifth, nor even with other small Eastern Township villages, such as Warden which was incorporated in 1795. Still, one hundred and thirty-five years was worth noting.

Not all settlements survive. The sculpted metal tree commissioned by the RCHS that stands behind the Melbourne Township Town Hall bears the names of some three dozen places that were once nascent communities in Richmond County but that no longer exist. Places like Lisgar, New London, and Upper Flodden had their own churches and schools and even train stations. They were small clusters of houses and sheds where tinsmiths, cobblers and coopers set up shop to serve the farmers who were clearing land, sowing crops and raising families in the immediate vicinity. At a time when, even after the revolution of the railway, distance was determined by how far a man could reasonably travel by horse and wagon, it stood to reason that one would find hamlets, villages and towns growing up within a relatively close proximity to one another.

But industry supplanted agriculture; the car replaced the horse. Surviving for one hundred and thirty-five years must be at least a minor accomplishment. And the truth is that the place is much older. Even though Richmond was incorporated as a town in 1882, the first settlers started building homes and barns at the site in 1798, arguably making it almost two hundred and twenty years old. Along the same vein, the name Richmond has been used to designate both the town and its hinterland since 1820. And while counties have been replaced by MRCs (Municipalités régionales de comté or Regional County

Municipalities), the name Richmond continues to designate both federal and provincial electoral ridings.

*The Annals* are a rather eclectic collection of related writings and, to some extent, this book might be described the same way. The pieces that make up this collection are all from the same pen, but saw light over a period of four decades. They form an anecdotal history in that there is a chronological thread to the stories but it's not a thread pulled taut and straight. To mix metaphors, if a formal history is a four-lane highway, this book is a meandering country road.

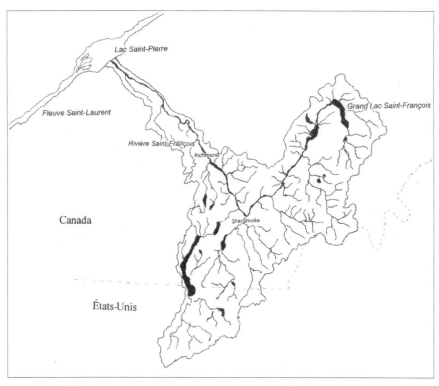

St. Francis Watershed: Political boundaries and roadways delineate our maps and our lives today. But it was the streams, brooks, and rivers that formed after the last ice age that defined the lives of First Nations people and the early Europeans.

# The River

"We wouldn't be here if not for the river."

Jacques Marin of *Action St. François*

THERE IS AN IRREFUTABLE LOGIC imposed on mankind by geography and history. The story of Richmond and its hinterland flows, figuratively and literally, from the St. Francis River, *la rivière Saint-François*. The geography drew the man, and the man created history. Without a river, without foothills, without vigorous vegetation, would that first man, and his family and clan and tribe, have had any reason to come and (much later) to settle here? Certainly when the first Europeans rushed to the St. Francis River Valley to take possession of arable acreage and river frontage, they came because they were being forced from their former homes by the recurring crises that make up history. But they came here because of the geography, and more particularly because of the river.

The St. Francis has a history of its own. It was formed some ten thousand years ago, a small scar left behind by retreating glaciers. It's a somewhat unusual river in that it first flows southwest out of Le Grand lac Saint-François for more than a third of its two hundred and eighteen kilometres before it abruptly makes a nine-ty-degree turn when it reaches Sherbrooke, and then flows north-west to its mouth at Pierreville, where it spills into the St. Lawrence. It has dozens of tributaries, of which the most impressive is the Magog River that thunderously joins it in Sherbrooke. It has a watershed that spreads over ten thousand square kilometres, roughly ten percent of which lies in the United States.

For most of its ten or twelve thousand years, the river evolved to the syncopated rhythms imposed by the seasons. In the spring, ice break-up, rainfall and snowmelt would cause the unfrozen river to rise and flow more quickly. In places it would scour its banks, stripping away soil and vegetation; elsewhere it would surge over its banks and flood low-lying lands, depositing debris that ranged from tree trunks and boulders to the fine, nurturing particles that create rich, alluvial soils. Through the summer and fall, the land would grow dry. The rivulets, brooks, streams and creeks would grow smaller, sometimes disappearing altogether, and so the river would shrink, creating sandbanks and islands. Through the drier seasons there were occasional downpours that resulted in flash floods, but generally the river would flow almost placidly. After the fall rains came winter and the river would freeze over solidly for four or five months, some-times freezing to a depth of several feet. Then the spring sun would start the cycle again, provoking the ice to creak and groan and break up into pans the size of garden sheds that would be carried off by the floodwaters.

The river was far wider when it first formed. What is now the valley floor was originally part of the river bed; for part of its length the valley has provided a convenient place to lay down dirt roads, railway tracks, and four-lane highways. Escarpments rising steeply hundreds of yards from the existing river, gravel beds, and sand pits are all discreet indicators of just how wide the river once was.

Vegetation, fauna, and eventually humans all slowly moved onto the land liberated from its cover of ice. Exactly when First Nations people, or perhaps their predecessors, first walked along the banks of the river, or crossed it on a floating log, is not known, but there may have been small tribes of hunter gatherers coming into the area as long as five thousand years ago, or earlier.

The Abenaki, who are the First Nations people considered to be indigenous to the area, were actually recent arrivals. Like so many who came after them, the Abenaki were political and economic refugees. Originally they had lived along the northeastern seaboard of what is now the United States. As Pilgrims and other Anglo-Saxons fled religious persecution in England in the seventeenth century to settle in New England on the Atlantic seaboard, they inevitably encroached upon the Abenaki. Driven from their homelands by gunpowder and disease, the Abenaki were welcomed as allies by the French. In 1669, they were given two seigneuries along the south shore of the St. Lawrence: one at the mouth of the St. Francis River and the other at the mouth of the Bécancour River.

The Abenaki were a semi-nomadic people and for half the year, from late spring until early fall, they lived in small villages near the banks of the river where, in small clearings, they raised the three sisters: corn, squash, and beans. The river provided protein in the form of fish, including salmon, in bountiful supply. In the fall, the Abenaki would disband into family units and move inland to winter quarters where hunting would supplement the dried fall harvest. In canoes, the Abenaki moved up and down the river and its tributaries as need arose.

The recorded history of the St. Francis can be said to begin late in the seventeenth century when Jean Crevier built a small fort on the banks of the St. Francis near its mouth. The fort was erected in 1687, withstood Iroquois attacks in 1689 and 1693 before being largely destroyed by Rogers' Rangers in 1759. The fort was razed, but the people stayed. The Abenaki settlement of Odanak regrouped around the ruins of the fort; missionaries erected first a chapel and later a church, *Saint-François-de-Sales*.

Except for its mouth, the river was neither explored nor exploited by Europeans throughout the French Regime. Missionaries were sent west beyond the Ottawa River to save souls and become martyrs, and the *coureurs des bois* went that much further west and north in quest of the wealth promised by furs, but no one was encouraged to go south on the St. Francis. The foothills of the Appalachians, including the St. Francis watershed, were left untouched by the governors appointed in France to oversee what Voltaire described as *"quelques arpents de neige."* The lands south of the St. Lawrence Valley were left in their virgin state with the hope that the mountains and muskeg would act as barriers against possible invasion from the rapidly growing English colonies along the Atlantic seaboard.

As Abenaki raiders and Rogers' Rangers showed before and during the Seven Years' War, while generally effective, the barrier could be brutally penetrated, and occasionally was. Guy Moreau, in his book, *Histoire de Windsor*, points out that in 1690, François Hertel de Rouville used the river on his way to attack an English village on the Maine coast and his son, Jean-Baptiste Hertel, similarly used the river to launch an attack on Deerfield in Massachusetts in 1704.

The Abenaki called the river by two different names, Alsiganteku and Skaswantegan. The first name roughly translates as river of trailing grasses while the second means the place where we smoke. The former name seems a reference to the mouth of the river, where it meanders more sluggishly and provides a niche for aquatic weeds, while the latter is a reference to the summer meeting place at the juncture of the Magog and St. Francis Rivers.

Unlike other names, such as Memphremagog or Watopeka, neither Alsiganteku nor Skaswantegan fell with phonetic ease on French ears and in 1662 Jean de Lauzon, New France's fourth governor, named the river *Saint-François des Près* in honour of his oldest son, François de Lauzon, Lord of Lilet.

Even after the British victory on the Plains of Abraham in 1759, the river remained almost untouched by Europeans. The newly installed British Regime was otherwise preoccupied in the years immediately following the conquest, and by 1775, with the first shots of the American War of Independence, a vast barrier to the south of the St. Lawrence valley was again required. (This time it was Benedict Arnold who led an army down the Chaudière River to Quebec City to demonstrate the barrier's military failings.)

One of the first Europeans to paddle up the river in peace was a French-born, Harvard-educated, medical doctor who had a practice in Trois-Rivières. Pierre de Sales Laterrière had an adventurous streak and in 1786, prompted by curiosity, he paddled from the mouth of the St. Francis to the site of what is now Sherbrooke and was then an Abenaki summer village. According to Guy Moreau, he had been preceded by Noël Langlois and Pierre Abraham who, in 1742, had paddled upstream seeking wood for shipbuilding. (More than a century later, stands of white oak were razed to provide the British navy with the wood needed to build its fleets.)

At about the same time that Laterrière became the Eastern Townships' first tourist, in London, England, the decision was being made to start opening up the semi-permeable barrier to colonization. At the time, the name Eastern Townships designated a much vaster area than today, stretching from the Gaspé coast to the Richelieu Valley. The first section opened for settlement was ten thousand square miles that encompassed a large part of the St. Francis watershed. This wilderness was divided into one hundred townships, each of approximately one hundred square miles, and many but not all, drawn out as neat ten-mile by ten-mile squares, while others ended up as irregular polygons.

At the turn of the nineteenth century, surveyors including Jesse Pennoyer, Nathaniel Coffin, and David Kilbourne, set out to translate lines on paper into farmers' fence lines. They led survey teams that laboriously carted sextants, axes, chains and granite markers through virgin forest ahead of the first anxious settlers.

One of the first of these to arrive on the St. Francis was Gilbert Hyatt, a Loyalist who came north during the War of Independence, but who resolutely refused to settle with most of his compatriots in the Western Townships—the fertile lands of what is now Southeastern Ontario.

In the summer of 1792, even before he had legal title to the land, Hyatt rushed to Three Forks, the same place Laterrière had visited, and where the Abenaki had been pitching their summer quarters for decades. It was thanks to his friend Pennoyer that Hyatt knew exactly the land to which he wanted to lay claim. It was hilly, but fertile. The waterfalls on the Magog River promised more than adequate power for a grist mill and a saw mill. Finally, the St. Francis offered a reliable highway to ship goods to Quebec City and Montreal.

Hyatt was the leader of a first wave of several dozen colonists, but there were a great many others who followed him into the Eastern Townships. The river and its tributaries were invaluable to all. A small number were Loyalists fleeing to friendly territory, like Hyatt, but most of the American settlers who arrived in the late eighteenth and early nineteenth centuries are more accurately referred to as Late Loyalists. Already familiar with the climate and geography of eastern North America, they came from Vermont, New Hampshire and upstate New York, in part because the newly formed United States of America was in some way unsatisfactory, but primarily because the Eastern Townships promised an opportunity for better land and a better life.

The river and the streams feeding into it were the first places of settlement, the sites of choice. It was the waterways that provided the lifeblood of the earliest communities: food, power and transportation. The river and its tributaries teemed with fish, an invaluable food source for more than half the year. (It's worth noting that at least three streams that feed into the St. Francis are named Salmon Creek.) And, despite the possible damage caused by floods, farmers were glad to have riverfront hayfields that were annually enriched by floodwater.

While Hyatt and his group got to Sherbrooke by bushwhacking through forty miles of forest from Magog, other early settlers used the river to reach their new homes. Elmore Cushing, who settled in what is now Richmond in 1798, came upriver by canoe with his family while his men drove a few head of livestock along the riverbank. In 1802, William Cross settled a little ways downstream near the mouth of the Ulverton River. Despite its relatively small size, it was powering at least a dozen mills along its length before the end of the nineteenth century. Of these, only one is still standing, and today Le Moulin Blanchette, that once produced wool, serves as a tourist site.

The first cash crop that was produced and shipped downriver was potash, made from the residual ashes of hardwood trees. While navigable, the St. Francis was not without rapids and small waterfalls that required portages. It was easier to use the river in mid-winter when its frozen surface created a natural roadway for sleds. Still, within a decade, early trails on both banks had turned into rough roads.

Later, the river was used to float log booms to saw mills in Trois-Rivières or Quebec City. Faint traces of this trade can still be found on the river: pitons driven into bedrock along the bank; rusted, foot-long, bent bolts protruding half their length from weathered timbers that once were a cribwork used to anchor cables that controlled the log booms.

The river, for all its benefits, was also a barrier. It might be crossed on foot or sleigh in the winter, but otherwise the early settlers would have to swim across or build a raft and pole across. It's not known when the first enterprising settler built a scow and started ferrying people back and forth across the river for a small fee, but there would have been several who followed suit up and down the river, and for at least a few decades—much longer in some places—ferrymen had well-remunerated employment.

Scows were not without their shortcomings according to the seasons and the weather. A bridge was desired and the first one, the Aylmer Bridge, was built in Sherbrooke in 1837. The second was erected a decade later, in Richmond. It cost travellers money to cross these early bridges, as it had cost them to cross the river on a scow, but the wooden structures were covered and so protected from the elements. In the context of the early settlers who had to wait for less inclement weather, or for the river to freeze solidly, or for floodwaters to subside to cross from one bank to the other, a bridge that permitted a crossing at any time in any season represented a tremendous advance.

The river continued as it always had, freezing and flooding. In 1848, a year after the bridge in Richmond had been erected, one of its five spans was severely damaged by spring ice and needed repairs. The metal bridge built in 1882 to replace the aging covered bridge suffered the same fate as its predecessor; it was first damaged in 1887 and then, in 1901, it was swept completely away by ice. The private company that owned the bridge was pushed into bankruptcy. The two public bridges that serve Richmond now date to 1903, when the Mackenzie Bridge was opened, and to 1967, when the Coburn Bridge was built.

Today, there are three railway bridges and a dozen roadway bridges crossing the St. Francis.

It was in the nineteenth century that the river, after a hundred centuries or more of almost pristine existence, began to feel the effects of mankind's presence. These were relatively minor at first: a bit of pollution from tanners and tinsmiths, cribwork to anchor cables, the small amount of garbage and refuse that those early setters produced. But the small settlements grew. Small shops that produced goods by hand eventually gave way to factories and mills employing hundreds that mass produced and mass polluted. Sewage pipes serving increasingly large populations spewed their black water out of river banks and into the cleansing St. Francis. The river carried all away and continued flowing seemingly the same.

Then, at the end of the nineteenth century, the river was changed by human hands.

Water-powered mills had been built on the tributaries of the St. Francis from the time of Hyatt's arrival. Often, the enterprising settler would dam up a small stream, or brook, or creek to create a millpond to feed a waterwheel to provide the energy to grind corn, or to saw wood, or to card wool. Well before the end of the nineteenth century, dams had been built on a number of the river's major tributaries and, in 1895, what has since become the Domtar paper company began work on a dam to harness the St. Francis. The Kreuger paper company followed suit in 1901 and built a dam at Bromptonville, now a borough of Sherbrooke. Finally, in 1920, the Southern Canada Power Company, which was nationalized by Hydro Quebec in 1963, built a dam at Hemmings Falls in Drummondville.

The dams on the St. Francis were made possible not only by advances in engineering, but primarily because of the advent of practical electricity. In 1868, an English aristocrat, Lord Armstrong, installed a hydroelectric station on his country estate and brought electric power to all his buildings, from manor house to stables. He installed electric lights, electric heating, and even an elevator run by electricity in the manor house. Armstrong's demonstration was sufficient that by 1882 there were the beginnings of power grids in London and New York. The electrification of the globe had begun and, as the twentieth century dawned, the St. Francis was put to use creating electricity.

The dams put an end to both log booms going downstream for sale to sawmills, and to Atlantic salmon coming upstream to spawn in many of the river's tributaries. As the century advanced, the river was put under greater and greater stress. More industry and a growing population created more and more garbage, refuse, and pollution.

The river got something of a reprieve late in the twentieth century when municipalities began installing waste treatment plants to deal with black water, so that almost all cities, towns, and villages on the St. Francis and its tributaries are now putting clean water back into the waterways. (Water is deemed clean if it passes the trout test: a given number of trout in a specifically sized basin must survive for a set period of time for the water to be considered clean.) The Domtar paper mill that for decades sent frothy brown suds downstream was demolished and replaced with a much cleaner operation two kilometres inland from the river. A new consciousness mandated the maintenance of a riparian strip along its banks. Almost everyone stopped the practice of casually tossing garbage into the river.

The river is generally cleaner now in the twenty-first century than it was for much of the twentieth. Salmon have not come back, but there are almost fifty varieties of fish that can be found in the St. Francis. There are kingfishers, herons, and eagles that take up summer residence. The river is again being used by fishermen and, at least near Drummondville, swimmers. Paddlers,

in canoes and kayaks, have become a relatively common summer sight.

If we are closer, as a species, to living in harmony with the
river, we are still far from perfect. Dams create small thermal
pockets so that a few ducks and geese remain here year round
instead of migrating. Fertilizer run-off carries chemical cocktails
through rivulets, streams, brooks, and creeks into the river. A
plethora of medications administered by doctors and vets also
ends up, despite the settling ponds of sewage stations, in the
river.

Still, the river is here, and because of it, so are we.

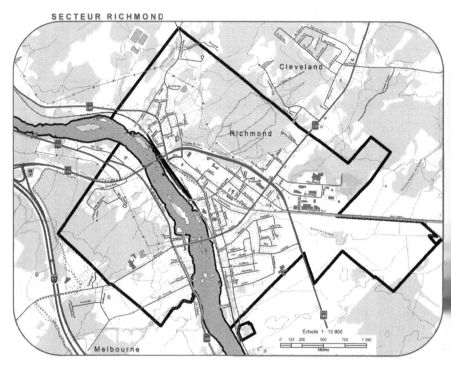

SECTEUR RICHMOND

Richmond Today: Political boundaries, even at the municipal level, can be quite inexplicably complex. The small imperfect square at the very bottom of the map is St. Anne's Anglican Cemetery, one of Richmond's extra-territorial holdings.
(MRC du Val-Saint-François)

# PART 1

# NOW: SNAPSHOTS OF RICHMOND

# CHAPTER 1

# A Town in Troubled Times

THE TOWN OF RICHMOND finds itself both bigger and smaller than it once was. As incorporated in 1882, Richmond was demarcated by the St. Francis River to the west and surrounded by the rural municipality of Cleveland, from which it was carved, on the other three sides. It grew by a half on January 29, 1999, when it absorbed the Village of Melbourne, which had at one time been its more prosperous sibling; the Village of Melbourne was incorporated before Richmond and, for a time, was more populous than Richmond. More recently, Richmond has been stretching a little to better accommodate its industrial park; parcels of a few dozen acres of contingent land have been acquired from Cleveland either by a monetary purchase or by a land exchange.

The boundaries that delineate the Town of Richmond form an irregular polygon with its share of acute and otherwise inexplicable angles. On the ground, where those cartographic straight lines are invisible, the result is not without some curious ironies. One is that Richmond Regional High School, erected in 1968, sits clumsily on the town's line; the building and soccer fields cleanly bisected. Another is that both at the north end and south end of the town are hayfields and pasturelands that lie within the Town's boundaries.

The Town of Richmond also has what might be called extra-territorial holdings. For example, St. Anne's cemetery rests entirely in Cleveland Township but is part of Richmond's jurisdiction. More significantly, the Town's water supply comes from a newly drilled well a few kilometres upstream, in Cleveland, while the Town's sewage treatment ponds are just downstream, in Cleveland, but on plots of land that belong to Richmond. (At one time, the Town owned a dam some thirty kilometres distant on Lake Brompton that served to control the water level of Salmon Creek, the source of the Town's drinking water at the time.)

Confined to a small territory (seven square kilometres), Richmond's population, now a little under 3200, has been as high as 5000, a number achieved when economic conditions were different and when families boasted many more children than they do today.

On Canada's one hundred and fiftieth birthday, Richmond's annual budget was just under five million dollars, a sum spent on road repair, snow removal, water treatment, garbage collection, police security and varying levels of financial support to different non-profit, community organizations that range from youth soccer to meals-on-wheels.

As is commonly the case with small municipal governments, Town administrators struggle to do all that is needed with the money available while homeowners complain that taxes are too high. In the case of Richmond, both viewpoints are justified. For the last several years the Town has been receiving an annual *péréquation*, an equalization payment disbursed by the provincial government to towns that are recognized as underprivileged.

Nowhere is the Town's status as underprivileged more evident than on Main Street.

Seen from any of the small aircraft that occasionally fly a few thousand feet over the town, especially during the summer on clear, sunny days, Richmond first appears like a carelessly thrown but comforting quilt: rooftops, treetops, a smattering of blue, sparkling pools. Then, very suddenly, the brightness below becomes barren: black tarred rooftops, strips and squares of asphalt, an uninviting no-man's land. A moment later the quilt is back, albeit only briefly. Then the town is gone and below flows the river through fields and forests cut by rail beds and roadways, and sprinkled with human habitats.

Richmond's Main Street, *rue Principale*, (or as it is sometimes heard to be called, Principale Street) is less dramatic when seen at ground level. Still, it is a noticeably unattractive downtown core. At the south end sits an oversized grocery store, finished in corrugated metal; the squat box is disturbingly similar to the railway box cars that roll by thirty metres away. Shortly after it was erected a decade ago, it earned the dubious distinction of being named the ugliest building in Quebec. But the grocery chain (and its uncompromisingly inexpensive design) was chosen over others because it promised the lowest prices, prices most likely to be within the range of affordability of the population to be served.

Richmond's *péréquation* is not newly won. Poverty has been with the Town for some time, if not from the very beginning. It is rare in human history that an accumulation of wealth by one individual or one group did not entail the impoverishment of others. During Richmond's early years, and before, there were benevolent societies, often church-based, that tried to ensure that those less fortunate had at least the bare necessities to remain alive. Today the Town acts, to the extent that it can, to help that percentage of the population that lives below the poverty line, citizens who survive from one welfare payment to the next. Besides an active participation in the Christmas Basket Campaign, the Town has been administering some three dozen subsidized housing units erected about twenty years ago by the provincial government. (The task is scheduled to be transferred soon to another administrative system.) There is always a waiting list for these apartments as their rental fee is set at twenty-five per cent of the occupant's income. The lower one's income, the more attractive subsidized housing is. For a single person living on a monthly welfare cheque of eight hundred dollars, an *Office municipal d'habitation* apartment is a boon. The units are located in three different buildings set in residential neighbourhoods.

But, for every individual fortunate enough to find subsidized housing, there are at least two or three others searching for the cheapest rent possible. Virtually all of those cheap rents are to be found on Main Street, a short walk from the big box grocery store.

# CHAPTER 2

# Christmas on Main Street

THE CHRISTMAS LIGHTS have already been up for a while on many of the homes in the residential areas. Sometimes it's just a string or two of artfully placed lights, sometimes it's an overabundance of energy-draining bulbs accompanied by a yard-full of inflatable plastic decorations. But not on Main Street.

This is a Main Street that has seen better days. Lots left empty by buildings lost to fire or old age remain empty. Sometimes it's just the apartments upstairs that bring in revenue; the store-fronts remain vacant despite the 'for sale' or 'for rent' signs. There are still a few dozen businesses (some of them doing well) along the three-block stretch of the downtown area, but there are also buildings that once bustled with commerce and are now residential units.

There are very few Christmas lights on Main Street; none on the building where Len and Tracy live; but then, all the other apartments in the building are vacant.

"There'll be three of us," says Len. "We'll have a fondue. We're going to celebrate on the twenty-fourth."

"I'm working on the twenty-fifth," says Tracy. "It's going to be just another day. We're not putting up a tree but we do exchange presents between ourselves."

"Although the present is never really a surprise," adds Len, "because we always check what the other person wants."

It's estimated that in North America up to twenty percent of the presents purchased at Christmas go almost directly into the garbage.

Len and Tracy couldn't afford a mistake of that magnitude. They live on about one thousand dollars a month which comes in part from Len's Quebec pension (he's sixty-three) and in part from Tracy's nine-dollar-per-hour job. They pay just over four hundred dollars per month for a five-room apartment. They don't own a car. At different times over the last several years, either one or the other has had recourse to welfare. Some years, they've asked for a Christmas basket and some months are more difficult than others.

It wasn't always so. At one time, for Len, money was plentiful.

"I was born in Denmark," he says. "My mother was a war bride and my father was in the air force. I was eighteen months old when I came to Canada and I've lived in practically every province in the country as my father moved from one base to another. At one point, he was stationed in France, and rather than send me to a Department of National Defence school, my mother sent me to live with one of my uncles in Denmark and I went to school there for four years. I'm bilingual, but in English and Danish."

Len graduated from high school twice: once in Denmark and a second time in Ontario. While still in his teens, he enlisted in the army where he spent two years.

After his stint in the military, he found work as a car mechanic. A few years later, he set his sails on a different course and started selling insurance, a job at which he proved to be more than proficient. He found time to enrol at York University where he earned a degree. He rose into management positions. He also started dabbling in real estate with fortuitous timing; the Toronto real-estate boom made him a millionaire.

"My second wife was from St. Felix de Kingsey," he says, "and, at a certain point, we bought a nice place on five acres of land. I also bought a small company that manufactured hi-tech equipment for geological surveying. I moved the company here, to Richmond, and things went well for a time. We were selling products to Norway, Germany, Australia, and even to the United States Navy."

Then an oil crisis suddenly caught Len unawares. Unable to get the financing he would have needed to stay afloat, the company went bankrupt, as did Len. That was just over a decade ago. Since then he has worked at a variety of odd jobs and today he describes himself as semi-retired.

"In retrospect," he says, "I think that if I'd moved my company across the border to Plattsburg—which I seriously considered doing—I might well still be in business. I opted not to. It's one of those mistakes we sometimes make in life."

"I'm not whining or complaining," he continues. "You play the cards you're dealt. I had a very interesting life—I did a lot, I travelled, I met very interesting people (including Christopher Plummer; I was an extra in a film called Highpoint in which he starred). I have no trouble accepting where I am today. In the summer I grow asparagus on a small plot behind the building. I look after my houseplants, I read, someone occasionally brings me a computer that needs looking at. I've been working on a cookbook which I hope to have on the Internet early in the new year.

"As far as Christmas goes," he says, "I think it's about kids. I grew up an only child and I have wonderful memories of Christmas, of going out carolling, of making presents for a gift exchange. I'd say that today Christmas is too commercial; stores start playing Christmas music far too early."

What, Len was asked, would he wish for if he could be granted one wish?

"Only one?" he says with a laugh.

He pauses a minute and then adds, "World peace?" but he's chuckling as he says it.

"At my age, what would I wish for?" he asks rhetorically. "Money is not really any longer important to me. For Tracy, perhaps. Although even then, for Tracy, what I really wish is for a family reconciliation, something that I couldn't buy for her regardless how much money I had.

"No," he says finally, "I don't really have any aspirations left and I can't really think of anything I'd want to have for Christmas."

Eight years after Len and Tracy told their story, their address is still Main Street, Richmond, but they've moved half a kilometre north, out of the Town's commercial core, to a nicer apartment not far from St. Bibiane's Church.

# CHAPTER 3

# The Women of Main Street

THAT MAIN STREET is impoverished is clear to see, but that is not the commercial core's only distinguishing feature. The other notable aspect of Richmond's Main Street is not evident to a visitor passing through, nor even necessarily to people who live in Richmond. This snapshot of Main Street is dated 2010.

Main Street is gap-toothed and even though a number of storekeepers have refurbished their storefronts, the term seedy still suggests itself. Yet, there are changes on Main Street even if the most significant change has been gradual and is not immediately apparent—and that is the change in ownership of those stores on Main Street.

"I'll have to get back to you with the exact numbers," says Guillaume Lyrette, the recently elected president of the Richmond Chamber of Commerce. "We have about ninety members and most—but not all—of the town's merchants belong to the Chamber of Commerce. But in effect, many of the stores on Main Street are now owned and operated by women."

The presence of women merchants is a step in the evolution of a society that has changed significantly in terms of gender equality over the last several decades. Historians point to WWII as a key factor that led to women entering the workplace. When the men went off to war, workers were needed both in the fields and on the factory floor. When the men came home from the war, the women didn't necessarily want to give up their pay-cheques and the perks that came with their jobs. A quarter century later, what was called the Women's Movement formalized an acceptance of a new status quo; at least in theory an equal access to economic opportunity.

In some areas, as in some places, employment equality may have taken a little longer. Then again, in some areas, male to female ratios have now been totally reversed. For example, a generation ago, women principals were few and far between; today a list of principals from virtually every school board in the country will show a marked preponderance of women.

"Women have been competing with men on the job market for quite a while," Guillaume points out. "They may have started at the bottom—minimum-wage jobs on a shop floor, or a clerk behind a counter—but they realized that they could do as well as men. It was the next logical step to go from store clerk to store owner.

"For my part," he continues, "I'm glad to see women on Main Street. Women often tend to make things happen. They bring new ideas, and also a different attitude. They often have another set of values which go beyond the bottom line. They have to make money—every business does—but they don't make money their only consideration, or—at times—not even necessarily their primary one."

Guillaume concedes that Richmond's *rue Principale* is not an attractive street. "We are working at it," he states. "The Chamber of Commerce wants to work at making shopping in our own home town a reflex action. If more of us shop here, it will make it that much easier for shopkeepers to beautify their storefronts. The growing number of women owners will certainly help. Women often have a very good eye for detail, for making things more attractive."

Like all small towns, Richmond has been adversely affected by increasingly easy access to larger centres such as Drummondville and Sherbrooke. Accustomed as we are to overusing our cars, many of us have the reflex of ignoring the stores in our own towns and shopping farther from home.

"It's something that can change," Guillaume contends. By way of example he cites a local accountant who, until recently, always went to a large box store for all his stationery supplies. Today he buys the paper, pens, and ink cartridges he needs on Main Street in Richmond.

"He may spend a few cents more on certain items," Guillaume concedes, "but he is saving on gas and saving on time. Even items which might not be in stock in a small store can easily be ordered."

One of the many women merchants on Main Street is Michelle Nadeau who owns Papeterie 2000 Richmond. "If you're looking at women owners, I'm probably one of the senior members," she says with a smile as she starts her story.

"I was over fifty when I opened the store," she says. "I had no previous background in retailing but I sensed that running a stationery store was something that I could do. I knew a lot about office supplies because I had worked for sixteen years in the office of a notary, René Thibeault, who died prematurely (and who is remembered by the small urban park just north of where his office once was). I found work in a lawyer's office, but I discovered that there was quite a difference between the clients who went to see a lawyer and those who went to see a notary. I then went to work for another notary, but the office was in Sherbrooke, and after six months I just didn't want to keep doing the daily drive."

That was fourteen years ago. Today, Michelle has a junior partner—her daughter, Manon—and one employee. The store offers a number of services including printing. Business, Michelle will tell you, is good.

For the last three decades business has similarly been good for Manon Morin, whose florist's shop is just two doors down. "This is one of the oldest women-run businesses on the street," she says with a laugh. "My father bought the business thirty-three years ago with a partner. I was in high school and I worked here part time and in the summer. Two years later, after finding out I didn't really want to pursue translation—which is what I had set out to study when I started Cégep—I came back. My father's partner was leaving the business and I've been here ever since.

"It was hard at the beginning," Manon acknowledges. "I was young. There was another florist in town. It also takes time for any business to get going. I have one employee who has been with me for twenty-eight years."

Like Manon Morin, Erika Lockwood also laughs when she mentions that she's the oldest experienced bar owner on Main Street. (There are four bars on the three blocks that make up Richmond's downtown core, of which two—including the one featuring dancers—are owned and operated by women.) A native of nearby Danville, Erika started university expecting to embark on a teaching career. After her first work-placement in a local English school, she sat down to reconsider her options— one of which led her to purchase the Grand Central Hotel, better known as Gunter's, and considered by many to be as much an institution as a bar.

"I started working for Clifford Gunter about ten years ago," Erika explains. "For decades this had been a men only tavern and I was the first woman to work here behind the counter. It was a challenge at first but I take a certain amount of pride in having been the first.

"One day I came to work," she continues, "and saw a huge For Sale sign on the end of the building. I told Cliff that if he didn't take the sign down, I was quitting. I've owned the hotel for seven years now. I normally have four or five employees on staff and I work in here about fifty to sixty hours a week. The place still looks old, dark and antique-like, but for some of our regular customers, it's a little like a living room. Since I took over there has been a shift in both the age and gender ratios of my customers.

"This is my place," she states, "and I believe in it. I believe in Richmond and I do a certain amount of volunteer work, both with the Saint Patrick's Society and with the Richmond Fair.

"I'm lucky," she continues, "in that my character fits my work. Business is good, but it's also a challenge. Every time I look up there seems to be a new law to comply with. We were affected by the no smoking law and we'll be affected if the blood alcohol level for driving is changed. Recently I had to take a sixteen-hour course on serving food. We don't serve food, but the Tavern has always sold pickled cheese, and if I wanted to continue selling it, I had to take the course."

Another young woman who is taking over a place which is as much an institution as a business is Julie O'Donnell who, in 2008, became part owner of Quincaillerie Richmond Hardware.

As was the case for Erika Lockwood, a young woman behind the counter of a traditionally male business ruffled a few male feathers. "It happened a few times," says Julie, "that someone wanted to be served by Paul or Mark. On a few occasions the customers ended up being served by me and they were surprised that I could help them just as much as my uncle or my father."

If Julie is comfortable in Richmond's best-loved hardware store, it's in part because, despite her young age, she has already spent a lot of time there. "I started working here during my summer vacations when I was about fourteen," she says. "After I graduated from Mont Notre-Dame, the private girls' school in Sherbrooke, I went to Ottawa to follow a two-year cooking program. By the end of my first year I realized that I didn't want to be a cook. Still, I finished my second year to get my diploma and then I started working here.

"After a year in the store I realized that this is where I wanted to be," she continues. "I'm from Richmond. This is home. I like the store and it feels good to be here. Family certainly played a role in my decision."

The store that Julie now partly owns has been in the O'Donnell family since her uncle Paul bought the place lock, stock and barrel in 1978. A year and a half later, Julie's dad, Mark, joined her uncle in the business. Of course, what is now the O'Donnell store has been selling hardware since before living memory.

"Before us," explains Mark O'Donnell, "the store was run by Barry Armitage and Lawrence Rodgers. They had taken over from Bruce Bailey who in his turn had bought the store from the Bidgood Brothers. Before them, it belonged to Ginn and Elliot. Julie is another generation and she's bringing in new blood and new ideas."

When people new to the area discover Richmond Hardware, they invariably marvel at the store, or at least at the social role that the store plays. It's a place where people are likely to come in and chat, but more than that, the store serves as what might best be called an information exchange. For advice on some little job around the house, or to know where So-and-so is now living, or who to call to get almost anything under the sun, it's the place to go.

"We have contact with a wide spectrum of people," explains Julie. "I can't explain it more than that, but that is part of what makes it fun."

Almost across the street from Richmond Hardware is Aux P'tits Oignons, a new grocery store which is similarly co-owned by a daughter-father team: Danièle and Pierre Normandin.

"My mother's not always here in the store," says Danièle, "but she's handling all the accounting and bookkeeping, so really there are three of us, plus one employee we recently hired."

Originally from Montreal, Danièle was introduced to the area when her husband chose the Université de Sherbrooke to follow a Master's program in Environmental Studies. "We knew we wanted to stay in the general area," she explains, "and a friend of mine suggested we look in Richmond where housing is much more affordable. We bought a place in Janesville which we're now fixing up.

"For me," she continues, "Richmond is like living in the country, like being in a village. Everyone knows everyone else. It's a welcoming, friendly place.

"I decided to open this store in part because I was surprised that Maxi was the only place in town to get fruit and vegetables, but also because I always wanted to have a fruit store. Before I embarked on the project, I spoke with a few people, including Annick Gélinas who recently opened La Bouchère du Village on College Street, and everybody was encouraging."

Barely a month after opening, Danièle describes business as increasing slowly but surely. "I have had people come in and tell me they'll never come back, but I also have regular customers who are coming in two or three times a week. In French 'aux p'tits oignons' is an expression which means to look after people. I think we're filling a need. We sell both regular and organically grown fruit and vegetables. We can't compete with the box store on prices, but we do offer a good variety of fresh, good quality produce. We also prepare soups, salads and vegetable lasagna on site; if we don't carry something you want, we'll order it for you."

Danièle estimates that it will take two years or more to reach the break-even point. "We're paying our bills, and the salary of one employee," she says. "Neither my parents nor I have started drawing a salary yet, even though I'm probably in here fifty or sixty hours a week. I feel confident about this project because I feel a lot of support from the community."

If Danièle Normandin is—for the moment—the newest woman on Main Street, Gisèle Leclerc is one of the most established. Owner of Boutique Gisèle, a women's clothing store, she opened her doors in 1973. "I moved to Richmond when I married," she says, "and I opened the store about twenty years later. I had no background in retail and I knew nothing about running a store. It was something I wanted to do. A clothing store was a natural choice. I'm not a clothes horse myself, but I have always loved good clothes.

"I started small and a number of years ago I enlarged the store, increasing my floor space by about fifty percent," she says. "As I recall, business was quite good from the start. It continues to be good. I hadn't really thought about it before, but today, there really are quite a few women running businesses on Main Street. It wasn't like that when I opened my store."

Indeed, when Gisèle Leclerc opened her boutique, there were half a dozen businesses on Main Street run by women—and this at a time when there were almost twice as many stores open for business. In the early 1970s, women-run businesses on Main Street had a decidedly feminine flavour. There was a very popular restaurant, Chez Thérèse, which was owned and operated by Thérèse Gagné. There was also Repas Minute Lunch, a small *cantine* or food stand run by a young woman named Réjeanne Roux, who, after fifty-six years in business, still owns and operates what is now Repas Minute Richmond and who still goes in to work at half past five in the morning, seven days a week. There were Jeannine Topping and Joanne Barbeau, both of whom owned small stores that sold women's clothing. There was also Liliane Comeau and her daughter, Jeannette Charland, who could be found behind the counter at Magasin Comeau, a store that sold fabrics and the accoutrements of sewing.

Today you're likely to find Anne-Marie Charland, Jeanette's daughter, behind the counter of Magasin Comeau. "Business today isn't what it was," she says, "and that's because at one time many if not most women sewed at least some of their own or their children's clothing. There are still women who sew and come in here to buy material for blouses or curtains, but not as many as a generation or two ago. Still, the store is doing fine."

Almost across the street from Magasin Comeau, after sitting empty for quite a while, what used to be the Dollar Store is undergoing extensive renovation and some beautification. When it opens it will house Maison Cannelle, owned and operated by Elizabeth Dupont whose specialty kitchen prepares gluten-free and lactose-free foods, which are distributed and sold through-out much of the province. For the last several years, Maison Cannelle has been operating across the river on Bridge Street, in a building that can no longer accommodate an expanding enterprise.

"We plan to open on Main Street on July 27," says Elizabeth Dupont. "In all, the new building has about twenty-five hundred square feet of floor space. There will be a bakery in the back, and in the front we're opening a small café which will offer desserts. At present I have a dozen employees, of whom five will be working on Main Street while the others will continue to work at the original place on Bridge Street."

If you drive downriver along Richmond's Main Street, the first business you'll see is Repas Minute Richmond, Réjeanne Roux's small *cantine*. The last storefront you'll pass as you head out the north end of town towards Trenholmville is L'Univers Esthétique, recently opened by Christine Mayette. In between, of the twenty-eight storefronts on the street, eighteen are owned—in total or in part—by the women of Main Street.

Just to say how quickly, or perhaps slowly, a town evolves, in the seven years since that piece was written, the following changes have taken place: the president of the Chamber of Commerce is now a woman, Hélène Tousignant; Danièle has gone out of business and the store she occupied now sells used clothing; l'Univers Esthétique has closed; Elizabeth moved into her store on Main Street and then out again in favour of a much larger facility in the industrial park where she concentrates on baking. The number of bars has dropped from four to three; the building where dancers used to perform now belongs to the Comité de promotion industrielle de Richmond, making it, in effect, a municipal building. Curiously, it still operates sporadically as a bar. The building faces onto Parc René-Thibault and, on occasions such as *les vendredis en folie* when there's live entertainment and a crowd of people, non-profit organizations raise funds by selling beer and soft drinks from a side entrance.

Under water, 1906. This group seems more interested in the camera than the flooding, which was an annual occurrence. Note the bracing to help support the wall of the adjoining building. Note, as well, the electric wires; the surrounding countryside would not have electric power till the early 1950s. (RCHS Archival Collection)

CHAPTER 4

# Gunter's

B EER IS A POPULAR COMMODITY on Main Street, and long
has been. Of all the business establishments in Richmond's
commercial core, none has been operating longer than Erika
Lockwood's Grand Central Hotel, better known as Gunter's.
It's been selling beer for well over ninety years as it was a hotel
before it became Gunter's.

The following piece can perhaps serve as a stepping stone
towards the past. It was published in the *Sherbrooke Record* on
March 28, 1979, almost four decades ago. Gunter's today is recognizably the same but also noticeably different. Today, two of
its three stories sit empty; its vocation curtailed. Its kitchen,
once relatively renowned, is no more. And of course, the Gunter
brothers, Cliff and Doug, owners for half a century, are now
deceased.

*The Office*

> "A businessman who wants to succeed in Quebec need only open a feed mill or tavern."
>
> *Anonymous*

Cliff Gunter Jr., who, along with his brother Doug, owns and operates the Grand Central Hotel concedes that there may be some truth to this maxim.

"The hotel gives us a pretty good living," he says. "It was tough going when we first took over but for the last few years it's been a lot easier. We can sit back a little more and we don't have as many worries as we used to."

While the Grand Central is the official name of the hotel, it is most commonly called "Gunter's" or "The Office." The latter moniker is a throwback to the days when farmers and auctioneers, lumbermen and Christmas tree buyers, would sit down at a booth for a little business before a little pleasure.

In contrast to the heyday of the railway when as many as six passenger trains a day rolled through Richmond, the hotel's rooms get very little use these days. "We have a handful of permanent guests," explained Cliff, "and occasionally a journeyman who will stay a month or two while he has a job in the area. The rooms are no longer the bread and butter of the hotel; we don't really do any more than break even on them."

While lodging is no longer a profitable venture for the hotel, the grill and tavern part of the operation do, as they always have done, a steady and even roaring trade.

"The amount of beer we sell varies a lot," Doug explained. "On the average we sell some ten to twelve barrels of draft beer a week. At twelve-point-seven gallons per barrel that's about one hundred and fifty gallons of draft a week, plus of course the bottled beer and the hard stuff."

Holidays are when the hotel does its best: one day last Christmas Gunter's sold one hundred and ninety-seven dozen bottles of beer.

While the quantity of brewed potables sold seems prodigious, it must be remembered that Canadians are a breed apart when it comes to consuming beer; last year [1978] we poured about two billion gallons of the stuff down our gullets. Richmond too is probably a town apart when it comes to beer; despite a population of less than four thousand, the Town lays claim to no less than eight drinking establishments.

Over the last several years, as fashions and trends from the big city have filtered through the province, a number of Richmond's hotels and bars have tried various gambits to entice more customers to enter their doors. For a while, a couple of the hotels offered live bands, another installed a discotheque, a few tried go-go girls and strippers (male as well as female) and one bar is currently featuring X-rated films on closed-circuit TV. Gunter's Hotel stayed a step ahead of the competition with what it has always offered: good service, clean floors and a friendly, even homey, atmosphere.

With the exception of Sunday, when it stays closed, the Grand Central opens every day at eight in the morning. While most of Richmond's population prefers orange juice or coffee at this early hour, the shop-workers coming off the midnight shift at Kingsbury like to drop in and unwind with a quart or two of beer. The early morning habitués also include hotel guests, who spend the morning playing gin rummy rather than drinking.

"Gunter's is an amazing place in the morning," one regular customer explained, "It's almost like a gentleman's club you'd read about in a nineteenth-century English novel, except you see workmen instead of aristocrats. But it has the same feeling—quiet, calm, peaceful co-existence."

As the morning wears on the tavern seems to draw more people. At noon, especially during the warm weather, locals like to drop in for a quick cold one or perhaps a few drafts and a bit to eat—a meal euphemistically called a liquid lunch. The menu today is limited: a few varieties of pre-packaged sandwiches, chips, salted peanuts, and pickled tongue, cheese or eggs. The fare is humble, but nevertheless makes for an enjoyable meal.

During the afternoon the grill, which is always darker and cooler than the tavern, begins to draw people, usually couples. [Women were not allowed in the tavern until the mid-1980s.] Old friends pass the time over a card game or possibly over the bumper-pool table. An errand downtown is often an excuse to drop into Gunter's for a draft and a chat.

An evening at Gunter's can be calm or hectic, depending on the day of the week. Monday and Tuesday nights are quiet; on Wednesday night the dart players take over the grill and spill into the tavern. Thursday is payday in the local shops and Gunter's is transformed into a noisy, hectic, almost chaotic place. On Friday and Saturday nights the hotel is invaded by a younger crowd—the kids home from Champlain Cégep and Bishop's University.

If Gunter's has a unique atmosphere, the reason probably lies in the history of the hotel. Like all of Richmond, the hotel's roots are closely linked to the Canadian National Railway. 'Uncle Jim' Gunter, the grandfather of the present owners, was a railroad man turned innkeeper; Cliff Gunter Sr., the father of the present owners was also a railroad man. And until the 1950s, when the car replaced the train as the most popular means of transportation, the Grand Central Hotel owed its prosperity to the railway.

"The hotel was bought by our grandfather, James Steven Gunter, in 1925 for seventeen thousand dollars," explained Cliff. "He was born in South Durham in 1868 on a farm that stayed in the Gunter name until just last year. He was one of seven brothers, all of whom went on to do quite well. He worked as a farmer, and as a railway man, and when he lost an arm in an accident, he launched himself into the hotel business."

Although Jim Gunter went on to make a small fortune in a variety of business ventures, his first year as a hotel keeper was a disaster.

"He went bankrupt," Cliff recounts. "To keep the hotel afloat he sold shares to his wife, to his brother Donald, and to my father. After that, he and his brother Donald ran it until 1947, when my father took it over."

Jim Gunter is still remembered by many people in and around Richmond. During his ninety-three years he managed to pack in a lot of living. "He was a very active businessman," Cliff explained. "He owned several farms and bought a great deal of land in the area, timbered it, and sold it off again. He made a lot of money but he also spent a lot. He was extremely sociable and he loved to have people around him and he was very generous with his money. It was very hard during the Depression but if a friend needed a loan, Uncle Jim was always there to help him out.

"Jim Gunter was also a character. One story I remember about him goes back to his days on the farm. He was selling hay to Montreal in those days and on one occasion felt he got short changed. The next year he got an order from the same fellow. Having lost money once, he wasn't going to let it happen again, so he went all around South Durham picking up the hay from chicken sheds. The hay was full of manure and therefore rather heavy. He covered it all with good hay and shipped it off. The irony in the story is that today, chicken manure is used in cattle feed to boost the protein content."

Art Fowler, who has known the Gunter family all his life, tells another anecdote of Uncle Jim. "This story goes back some seventy-five years. Jim got into a dispute of some sort over a line fence with one of his neighbours. The two decided to settle it by putting up a gate; each man was to stay on his own side. When the gate was put up the neighbour leaned over it. Jim hauled off and hit him; he was a real fighter."

The hotel was a far different one when Jim Gunter ran it. The bar was more of a sideline and, the Gunter clan of that period being a rough-and-ready bunch who looked upon drinking and fighting as the best of entertainment, it soon earned itself a reputation. "There were fights in here all the time," Cliff explained. "The place was known as the Bucket of Blood.

"Whenever there was an argument, they'd have a fight to settle it. The two would go outside, have their scrap, come back in, shake hands and have a beer and be the best of friends."

Although the hotel never again went into bankruptcy after 1926, it was nevertheless run badly. "It was a good hotel but the grill and tavern were costing money rather than making it. My grandfather and his brother would think nothing of opening the bar up for a couple of hours at a time and offer free drinks to anybody who came in. At least once they had a party or celebration of one kind or another and the bar was open for a twenty-four hour stretch."

If the grill and tavern of the Grand Central Hotel were wild and woolly, the rest of the hotel was a rather classy establishment. "The hotel ran a buggy service to the train station," Cliff recalled. "There were six passenger trains a day stopping here in those days. The buggy would go down with guests leaving for Montreal or Quebec or Sherbrooke and come back with people from those places who had business here. Our cook, Lee Chou, who was with us for twenty-four years, would often prepare exotic specialties. He could send an order to Montreal for fresh lobster in the morning and get it that afternoon.

"Room and board cost four dollars and fifty cents a week in 1939. The hotel had a big kitchen—besides the cook there were three kitchen girls and another three chambermaids upstairs.

The hotel had a garage and a barn where we kept five sows just to reproduce enough pork for the kitchen. In those days it was common to serve one hundred meals at a sitting. During this era, Donald Gunter, Jim's brother, was elected president of the Hotel Association of Canada."

The physical appearance of the hotel has altered slightly over the years. Originally a wood frame structure, the hotel was given a brick facade in 1947 and the upper floor is in the process of being re-covered in aluminum sideboard.

"The floor in the tavern," Doug pointed out, "was unique in Canada when it was laid in 1925. It has lost some of its beauty over the years but has held up well. It's ceramic tile imported from Germany. We also used to have a magnificent table in here. It had been imported from Ireland and could easily sit a dozen people. We had to give it away when we moved a door from the corner to the centre of the far wall."

Over the years the hotel has faced both fire and flood. "We've only had one fire, in 1967," said Doug. "Nobody was hurt but we did have extensive damage in several of the rooms upstairs. We also had to rewire the hotel."

Floods have been harder on the building. Floods are an annual event in Richmond and, being located less than one hundred feet from the St. Francis River, Gunter's Hotel has seen and felt more than its share of floodwaters. "Every year, when the spring thaw comes, we get flooded," Cliff explained. "Usually it's just the basement and we spend three or four days pumping water. Other times however we get real damage. We've often ended up without heat or electricity because the water is so high."

The most memorable floods were those in the winters of 1927-28 and 1942-43. Doug recalled the latter flood, "My father came to get me in the boat. We rowed back to the hotel, tied the boat up to the veranda and we served beer from a room upstairs. The tables in the tavern were floating in five feet of water. We got it

BOATING THROUGH THE ICE AT RICHMOND, QUE. MARCH 28 1913

Boating through the ice, 1913. Looking almost triumphant, these boaters are making their way north on Main Street. The clock tower of the old Post Office appears faintly in the background.

bad but others got it worse. One business across the street had a plate glass window buckle and break under the pressure of the water."

Making the best of a bad situation, the regular patrons at the hotel started holding pools or lotteries every spring. As Cliff explained, "Every spring we'd try to guess to the exact hour the time the river would flood. Everybody would come in and place a buck or two with their guess. When the water reached a spot we had marked, we'd have a winner. We haven't done this for a few years but it used to be a regular event."

If Gunter's is unique in the Eastern Townships, it is undoubtedly because it is a family hotel. Until her death in 1952, Ada helped her husband, Jim, run the hotel and, since then, Marguerite, Cliff's and Doug's mother, has had a hand in operating the business. But Gunter's is a family hotel in more ways than one. The turnover in staff at the hotel is negligible—Les and Ellen Mummery, for example, have forty-eight years of service at the hotel between them. Patrons also tend to make the hotel a family tradition; fathers and sons often sit down together to share a beer and a conversation.

As an institution, Gunter's is probably a very accurate reflection of the fortunes of Richmond and the social mores of the three generations it spans. When Richmond was an active, booming town, the hotel was a rowdy, booming bar; today the hotel is as quiet and pleasant as Richmond is. Doug and Cliff will continue running the hotel for a while longer. Both have children and although it is too early to predict, it is possible that a fourth generation will continue with the business. In an age of change and transition, a few traditions at least should be maintained.

As we now know, the Grand Central Hotel was sold by Clifford Gunter, several years after his brother's death, to Erika Lockwood. The hotel didn't remain in the family for a fourth generation, but the place is still open, still called Gunter's, and still recognizably the same.

PART 2

# THEN:
# EARLY EUROPEAN
# SETTLEMENT

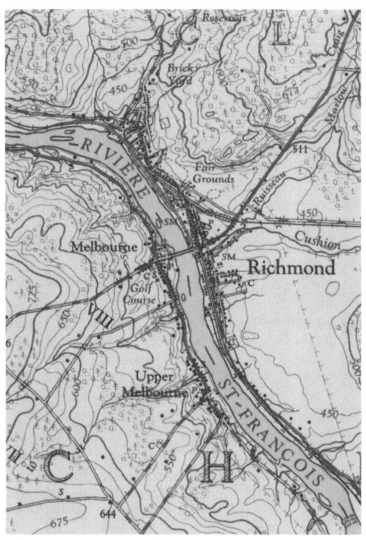

This topographical map prepared by the federal government might be quite accurate in most respects but Cushing Brook is incorrectly noted as Cushion Brook. How it became 'Cushion' remains a mystery.
(Bibliothèque et Archives nationales du Québec)

# CHAPTER 5

# Cushing Brook

THE RECORDED HISTORY OF RICHMOND and its hinterland begins with the arrival of Elmore Cushing. In the *Annals*, Alice Dresser describes him landing at the mouth of the brook that still carries his name on May 24, 1798. She depicts him arriving with his wife and family with Native Americans "in charge of the nine canoes, while two men drove the cow and oxen along the river bank." Within three months, Cushing had built a cabin, and four years later was operating both a saw mill and a grist mill.

A noteworthy narration of Richmond's earliest days comes from the Reverend Edward Cleveland, who in 1858 published a small volume entitled *A Sketch of the early settlement and history of Shipton, Canada East.*

Cleveland writes:

> The charter of the township was granted to Elmore Cushing and 46 associates in December 1801. In consequence of an offer from the Government of 1200 acres of land apiece to actual settlers, large numbers came from New England to this place when it was unbroken wilderness, and laid the foundations of many generations. But as they were poor and unable to fulfil all the conditions, the charter was delayed 4 years from the commencement of the

settlement; which led some to leave the place, and prevented others from coming.

The party that first entered the township to survey it, in 1797, were George Barnard, the manager, Prentice Cushing, and John Brockas, the chairman, Joseph Kilburn, the surveyor, and five Frenchmen, the axemen and packmen. They traced the outlines of the township, scaled the river, and ran a few concessions back that the associates might have opportunity to select one lot apiece to begin with. The survey was completed in 1801, by Christopher Bailey, from Vermont.

The following comprise most of the families who came previous to 1804: Elmore Cushing, William Runlet, James and Daniel Doying, Stephen Olney, David and John Harvey, Daniel Adams, Hosmer Cleveland, Nathan Williamson, Zepheniah Spicer, Ephraim Magoon, Stephen Daniels, Samuel Marstin, David Leviston, Charles Clark, Joseph Perkins, Jonathan Fowler, Jonas Clark, John Philbrick, Lot and Job Wetherall, John B. Labonte, the Hicks families, four in number, Isaac Burnham, the Drs. Silver, father and son, John Sweeney, Thomas Simson, William and John Lester, John and Nathaniel Piper, Stephen, George, and Henry Barnard, John Stephens, William Dustin, Royal and Joseph Shaw, Job Cushing, Samuel Smart, Joel Leet, Benjamin Andros, Timothy Morrill, Noah and Gordon Lawrence, John Smith, and perhaps some others.

Levi and A.R. Leet, Simeon Flint, John B. Emerson, Timothy Brooks, Benjamin Burbank, Solomon Daniels, Jesse Crown, Thomas Elliot, Nutting, Kezer, Woodman, Clough, Parsons, Richardson, Butler, Enoch Harvey, Solomon Emerson, Moses Hall, Burroughs, Healey, Mathews, Higby, Jared, Bray, Eber, Joseph, Benjamin, and Thomas Willey, Charles Bickford, Ezra Brainard, and perhaps a few others, came soon afterwards. These came from different States of New England, and prepared the way for the good that has followed. And it will readily be inferred that they were men of energy, courage, and large hope, to commence an enterprise so far in the wilderness, and attended with so much self-denial and hardship.

The first couple united by marriage in the township was Daniel Adams and his wife, who are now alive, the one 77 and the other 79 years of age, having lived to see their children to the fourth generation. Many other families have also become numerous. Lydia Doying, a daughter of Daniel Doying, was the first child born in the township. Her brother, Daniel, was the first male.

Who was Elmore Cushing, and why did he settle in what is now Richmond? Alice Dresser no doubt saw him as Edward Cleveland did, a man of "energy, courage, and large hope." In addition to the saw mill and grist mill that Cushing erected, he also built a pearl-ashery to further refine potash and a distillery that Dresser describes as "another necessity of those days." Dresser probably penned her portrait of Cushing early in the 1960s when the movement had largely died out, but she would have grown up acutely aware of and likely quite influenced by the Temperance movement that advocated strongly against all alcoholic beverages.

Dresser writes that, "Before coming to Shipton, Cushing had done his adopted country valuable service by giving testimony in the trial of David MacLean." (McLean was accused of fomenting a rebellion.) Intentionally or not, she goes on in such a way that the reader might wonder about Cushing's patriotism, "We may be sure that many people, loyal though they were, field a strong revulsion towards Elmore Cushing and the other two men whose testimony had delivered David MacLean to the unspeakable horrors of such a death." MacLean, she points out, "was hanged, drawn, quartered, and beheaded."

Several years after arriving in Shipton, in the years preceding the War of 1812-1814, Cushing became the commander of the first cavalry corps of the Eastern Townships. It is not clear if Cushing served in the war and it is quite possible that he did not. On March 27 of 1813, a year after burying his wife in St. Anne's Cemetery, Cushing resigned his post, abandoned his holdings in Richmond and moved to Montreal. His property was sold at a sheriff's auction.

A less nuanced description of Cushing comes from Joseph-Charles St-Amant, who in 1932 published a small tome entitled *Un coin des cantons de l'Est*. St-Amant identifies both Elmore Cushing and William Barnard as Americans who had acted as spies "*pour le gouvernement canadien* [sic] *durant la guerre de l'indépendance.*" He goes on to note that the two men were granted the townships of Brompton and Shipton as a reward for their loyalty.

*The Dictionary of Canadian Biography* states that Cushing was granted the Shipton Township for testifying, in 1797, against David McLean. While McLean was executed for treason, it is quite possible that he was an innocent American wood merchant, and that those who testified against him, did so for profit.

Whatever the case, Cushing is credited as Richmond's founding settler. At the time, settlement was being carried out by a system of leaders and associates. A promoter, or leader, would recruit a number of associates who were granted twelve hundred acres each in a designated township. Each of them would then give the leader one thousand acres to reimburse him for the cost of petitioning the government, conducting surveys, undertaking road building, and other such expenses.

Cushing is described as having been perennially short of cash, yet he seems to have done his share for the nascent settlement. He is said to have cleared twenty-four acres of land in his first year on the banks of the St. Francis and within the next few years he erected both a saw mill and a grist mill on the small brook that bears his name.

Today, someone paddling on the St. Francis and searching for Cushing Brook would be hard pressed to find it. Rather, the curious paddler would see, just upstream from the Mackenzie

Bridge, an eight-foot culvert. That culvert runs a few hundred metres or more back from the river and is buried deep under a set of railway tracks, under Main Street, under a large parking lot, under College Street, under a second, smaller parking lot, and under a stretch of green space before finally surfacing to receive the waters of Cushing Brook. A dozen or more home-owners along Stanley and Craig Streets can see the small brook running through their backyards. Otherwise, only a short stretch along the bicycle path offers a view of it today.

For Cushing and those who came to the Front Village of Shipton and the surrounding area during its first decade of settlement, travel was arduous at the best of times. Some settlers (like Captain John Savage who settled West Shefford—the area around Bromont—in 1792) made the trek north from Vermont and the New England states by tramping through swamps and hardwood forests. One attraction of Shipton at the turn of the nineteenth century was that it could be reached by water. Some, like Cushing, paddled up the St. Francis; others used tributaries and paddled downriver to get there. Yet others set off from Trois-Rivières and paddled up the Nicolet River to what is now the Danville area but was originally known as the Back Village of Shipton.

The waterways were used both in the summer and winter. For all the hardships posed by snow and cold, frozen rivers served as better-than-average roadways for sleds pulled by oxen. There were advantages to travelling in winter—at least if there was a welcoming cabin at the final destination.

The first settlers, to the extent that it was possible, made their homes along the riverfront, and this despite the fact that the river tended to flood in the springtime. Riverside hayfields—these existed at least into the first few decades of the twentieth century—yielded bumper crops year after year as the river continued to deposit rich, alluvial soil with each flood.

Looking back more than two centuries ago, life seems impossibly difficult for those early settlers. Not so for them. The forests of the Eastern Townships were no more intimidating than those of the New England states. If anything, the land might have been a little more accommodating; here the settlers found themselves in the foothills of the Appalachian Mountains that tower considerably higher south of the U.S. border. They were accustomed to eking out a living. Both river and forest provided relatively bountiful supplies of protein. Hardwood trees were cut and burnt to ash which was soaked in water and then packed into barrels and yearly brought to market, most often at Trois-Rivières, and sold as potash or pearl ash. This was the land's first cash crop.

(In 2017, potash brings to mind vast underground mines in Saskatchewan that feed the fertilizer industry. Potash is a white, alkaline salt that is water soluble and known chemically as potassium carbonate. In pre-industrial times it was made by tossing the ashes left by a fire into a large pot, soaking them in water, and then allowing the water to evaporate. The fine white residue was used as a bleaching agent as well as in the making of glass and in the manufacturing of soap. Pearl ash referred to pot ash or potash that had been further purified by heating in a kiln.)

Once cleared, the land could yield a good variety of grains, vegetables and fruit to complement the fish and venison that required only patience on the part of the fisherman or hunter.

Cushing spent fifteen years in the settlement he founded. His descendants stayed; one of his great-great-grandsons was Horace Pettes Wales, who died childless and left his estate to found the retirement home that carries his name.

# CHAPTER 6

# The Denison Family

Elmore Cushing and his forty-six associates—or those who actually made it to Shipton—were slowly but steadily joined by others who sought free land, or better land, and the promise of a new life. Some settled close to Cushing's nascent hamlet, others a little further into the hinterland. In 1800, Captain William Wadleigh settled on the east side of the St. Francis, some dozen miles downstream from Cushing's homestead. Wadleigh was married to Mary Blasdel, and shortly after their arrival, their son, Rufus, was the first non-native child to be born in the area. In 1802, another New Englander, William Cross, settled a half-dozen miles downstream from Cushing, on the west bank of the St. Francis. Just as Cushing's place became Richmond, so too Wadleigh's site grew into St. Félix de Kingsey, and the Cross homestead flowered into Ulverton.

Avery Denison was another New Englander whose homestead grew into a hamlet. Denison is particularly interesting, in part because his family story is considerably better documented than those of his local contemporaries, but also because of the tangible legacy left by his immediate descendants who followed in his footsteps.

Denison Mills grew into a hamlet, and then a village with a small Anglican church and its own general store and post office, before subsiding into a crossroads for a rather large number of permanent and summer homes, many of them lining *Lac Denison*—not a natural lake but an artificial one created to provide a steady and constant stream of water to power mills which have long since ceased operating, although one was refurbished by the writer, James Quigg, in the 1970s.

Denison met a tragic and untimely end; he has the sad distinction of being the first person laid to rest in the Danville cemetery. Denison's first log cabin—like those built by Cushing, Cross, Wadleigh and virtually all other early settlers—has long since been torn down. However, the house his eldest son constructed in the 1830s still stands.

Seen on a midwinter day in 2015, the house looks as if it might have settled itself a little deeper into its environment, which would not be surprising after almost two centuries. Then again, this might just be an optical illusion caused by waist-deep snowdrifts.

It sits with a quiet presence just above the McLaughlin Road. Its white stucco finish might camouflage it against the winter snow if not for the ox-blood shutters and the slate roof. It's not a noticeably old house, nor is there anything about its simple, functional lines that makes it easy to guess when it might have been built. Solid, square, sprawling at the back with a clapboard-finished summer kitchen, that in turn is further extended by a shed; it's a deceptively big house.

The front door of the house, almost certainly original, is four feet wide. The front entrance gives three options: to the left a multi-purpose room that includes a dining room table and was once the parlour; to the right a very comfortable living room; straight ahead are the stairs. These, like the front door, are not standard: the rise is very high, almost twelve inches, and the tread is rather narrow, perhaps six inches—roughly the opposite of the way stairs are normally built today with a wider tread and lower rise. The result is a very steep staircase; going up it feels more like climbing a ladder than a set of stairs. The window sills are almost two feet wide. The original floorboards are pine planks, some almost sixteen inches wide.

Today, the bathroom and kitchen are not unlike those in any other modern home except for the fact that even in these rooms there's a great deal of wall space covered in weathered barnwood. Save for those two rooms, most of the first and second floors are original, hardly changed from what they were almost two centuries ago. It's only the attic—a place that for a dozen years or so served as a schoolhouse—that has been refurbished: skylights, wood panelling; a modern, functional space.

Today Dominique Lebel and Valery Pigeon live in what is known as the Stone House with their three daughters. From 1982 till 1995, it was the home of Mario Verdon—a radio announcer, host, and TV personality whose mellifluous voice on Radio-Canada is still remembered, as Peter Gzowski's voice is remembered by CBC listeners. Originally though, it was a Denison house, built in 1831 by Simeon Minor Denison (1801–1865). The Stone House remained in the Denison family until 1981 when Marguerite Philbrick Denison left the house to spend the last years of her life in Richmond.

Exactly when Avery Denison (1775–1826) arrived in Shipton is unclear. According to family history, he arrived in 1797, before Cushing, having obtained a grant of five thousand acres from the government. *The Dictionary of Canadian Biography* casts doubt on this story and suggests that he purchased his land from Cushing at some time between 1798 and 1800. In 1801, Denison returned to the States, married Eunice Williams, and brought her to his new homestead in Shipton. Their first child, Simeon

Minor, was born in 1801 and three more children would follow: another boy, John Williams, and two girls, Malvina and Eunice. (The elder son carried the name of his paternal grandmother, Keturah Minor, while the second boy carried his mother's family name, Williams.)

No less than any other, and possibly more than some, Denison was hardworking and ambitious. At a time when a sixty-acre farm was considered to be a big operation, he acquired five thousand acres. He built a first home on his property before marrying and later, with a growing family, he constructed a second, larger cabin to accommodate his brood. His property was well-situated: roughly half-way between the Front and Back Villages of Shipton (Richmond and Danville) and just off the Craig Road which was built in 1810 and was part of the roadway running from Quebec City, the capital of Lower Canada, to Boston. Denison was more than a subsistence farmer, as he raised cattle—a high-end commodity—and built and operated a small distillery using potatoes to make what was likely a rather potent—and probably very lucrative—moonshine.

Around 1822, Denison transferred his property to his elder son, Simeon Minor Denison. Was this because, at age forty-seven, he had already reached the statistical lifespan he might expect? Or was it because, not unlike many farmers even today who retire in their early fifties, he was ready to turn responsibility over to the next generation, even as he continued to work on the farm? Even more than today, farming was very much a family operation with many hands making light work. It is also possible that there were legal or financial reasons that made it expedient to transfer the property.

Avery Denison met his end very tragically on June 28, 1826. He had brought cattle to market in Quebec City and was on his way home, near Trois-Rivières, when he was set upon by highwaymen and killed. His body was brought home and buried in Danville, his being the first burial to take place in the new cemetery.

Avery's oldest son, Simeon Minor Denison (1801–1865), was twenty-five when his father was murdered. He was already nominally the owner of the family farm. He very much followed in his father's footsteps. Just as his father had, Simeon took time to build a house before taking a wife. The house that Simeon built in 1831 is very much indicative of just how well Avery had done. Built three decades after his father first erected a rough wooden cabin, Simeon's stone house would have been, for his contemporaries, as spectacular as it was solid. While stone houses could be found in Europe and in the French *seigneuries* along the St. Lawrence, they were rather rare in the Townships. Only after the house was built did Simeon Denison wed Mary Moore.

It was Simeon who was most responsible for the growth of the hamlet of Denison's Mills. Using rocks cleared from the land, he built two dams on a stream running a few hundred yards below the Stone House. These dams—envisaged by Avery although built by his son—powered first a grist mill, that he built in 1850, and then a saw mill that he erected in 1858. The first dam also created a small lake, which is now surrounded by cottages, more and more of which are becoming year-round homes. Simeon also built a blacksmith shop and drew up plans for a cheese factory that opened a year after his death.

Simeon and Mary had three sons; it was Isaac, the middle son and a bachelor, who eventually took over the Stone House. Isaac's younger brother, Joseph Root Denison (1839–1915) and his wife Amelia Hunton built the Brick House just a few hundred yards below the Stone House, where the road forks. In 1875, Isaac, Joseph, and neighbours built a small chapel known as Holy Trinity Anglican Church. Joseph, in addition to running the farm, the mills, the blacksmith shop, and the cheese factory, also opened a small general store in the Brick House and ran the post office.

Joseph's son, William Simeon Denison (1868–1937) was the next generation of the family to live in the Stone House, although he didn't move into the house until he was middle-aged and widowed. William Simeon and his wife, Annie Haggart (1869–1922) raised fourteen children in what is known as the Brick House. The fourteen Denison kids had the rather unique experience of tramping daily to their uncle's house and climbing up to the attic to go to school. For a decade or so at the turn of the twentieth century, before the Little Red Schoolhouse was built, the attic of the Stone House served as a classroom.

William Simeon, who was a McGill-trained civil engineer, stayed in Denison's Mills to farm. It was in the last years of his life, when he was operating the farm with his sons, Bill (William John Denison, 1901–1963) and Avery (Avery Robert Denison, 1902–1977) that the house was wired for electricity. Muriel Denison (1904–1980) had married Stanley Hill, an electrical engineer. Drawing power from the dam that his wife's great-grandfather had built, he provided lights and power to the Stone House, the Brick House and half a dozen outbuildings a full generation before hydroelectric power came to the rest of rural Quebec.

The Stone House eventually went to William Simeon's seventh child, Avery, who, with his brother Bill, continued on with the family farm until the late 1960s by which time much had changed, especially in the world of agriculture. Farming, which had been the occupation of ninety percent of the population when the first Denison broke soil in the Eastern Townships, was, by 1970, a way of life for less than ten percent of the population. With no one in the family to take over the farm, it was sold in 1981. After one hundred and fifty years of continuous occupation by the Denison family, the Stone House passed on to other owners.

"We've owned it for several years," says Valery Pigeon who, in 2015, called the Stone House home, "but it's only in the last year that we've moved in permanently. My husband still spends a few days a week in Quebec City, but after using it as a summer and weekend home for the last five or six years, we were ready to make it our permanent home. It's a wonderful house.

"The girls especially like it because being here gives them the feeling that they're continuously on vacation.

"We have had some work done on the house," she says, "and we were very fortunate in finding Eddy Fowler and Paul Driver, who are exceptional craftsmen. We've also had work done on some of the outbuildings; four of the original twelve are still standing. Nick Mason, who is almost like an artist, has reanimated the stable, the henhouse and the hay barn."

When the Lebels walk across their fields and into the woods, they inevitably realize when they reach the limits of their property. "Brush and even mature trees have grown up around them," Valery says, "but the stone fences marking the property lines are still there."

The Denison name wasn't to be found on any of the mailboxes that began disappearing from the entrances of driveways in 2014. It's been a quarter century since Marguerite Denison left her house. Yet there are Denison descendants still living on the original Denison homestead. A few hundred yards from the Stone House, the Brick House, erected by Joseph Denison several decades after Simeon Denison built a house for his wife-to-be, is home to Kirk Robinson and his family. Kirk's ancestor, six generations back, was an ambitious, hard-working Late Loyalist by the name of Avery Denison.

CHAPTER 7

# Daniel Thomas

THE BEGINNING OF THE NINETEENTH CENTURY was pre-industrial; life was agrarian. Most men were farmers, or more accurately, farm labourers. The allure of the American continent was the tantalizing possibility of being a farmer, even if that meant felling forests with an axe to create fields; for a farmer, unlike his labourers, owned land, and land was wealth. The first settlers inevitably were men who sought to farm. But as farmers grew in number, others, who were not farmers, came to support them: labourers of course, like the two men who drove Elmore Cushing's livestock along the river bank, but also blacksmiths, sawyers, millers, grocers, doctors, cobblers, coopers, teachers. Notaries too were on that list.

In 1808, a decade after Cushing's arrival, an ambitious, vigorous eighteen-year old left his home in Woodstock, Vermont, and made his way to Stanstead, across the border in Lower Canada, and then to Melbourne, across the river from Richmond, where he lived the remainder of his life. His name was Daniel Thomas, and he was the area's first notary, possibly the first notary in the Eastern Townships. At a time when travel was slow and difficult, he travelled to all corners of the Townships to notarize deeds. Despite time spent away from home, he was very prominent in, and committed to, his community. When he died at what was then a relatively ripe old age of sixty-five, Thomas, whose grandson was the artist, Frederick Simpson Coburn, left a considerable legacy.

For one thing, he left numerous descendants. Thomas married four times, the first time when he was only twenty, and the last time, just two years before his death, when he was sixty-three. He fathered eleven children; six with his second wife, Hannah Tilton, and five with his Irish-born, third wife, Elizabeth Armstrong. The second to last of Thomas's eleven children, Laura Ann Thomas, was the painter Frederick Coburn's mother.

Where did Thomas glean his legal training? Had he perhaps worked as a clerk in a legal office in Woodstock? And what made him venture further north into Lower Canada and the Eastern Townships? None of this is clear.

But he was a man with an innate sense of leadership. He was known as Squire Thomas, "squire" being a term reserved for major landowners who enjoyed high social standing. That he was a Justice of the Peace would only have served to give more weight to the title. His great-granddaughter by marriage, Evelyn Coburn, in her book, *F.S. Coburn, Beyond the Landscape,* notes that he arrived suddenly and unexpectedly in a field, surprising a small group of men who were preparing to fight a duel. His unanticipated appearance put an end to the duel, and quite likely the dispute. According to Coburn, this was the last duel ever to be held on Melbourne soil. It would be interesting to know just when this incident occurred. (After a few centuries of popularity in Great Britain, duelling fell into disfavour in the nineteenth century and the last duel on the British Isles took place in 1852. Given that in Britain—and Lower Canada was very much a British colony—duelling was for gentlemen, a term that implied the younger sons of the well-to-do, it is rather remarkable that a small pioneer village like Melbourne where people were eking out a living would have men anxious to fight a duel.)

By the 1830s, Squire Daniel Thomas was settled and prosperous. He was also contributing to the growth—both spiritual and physical—of Upper Melbourne.

Europeans in the eighteenth and nineteenth centuries were God-fearing and church-going. European colonists in North America were no less so. This was true of the French-speaking *Canadiens* who lived along the St. Lawrence, as of the Americans who first filtered into the Eastern Townships, and those who then started coming from the British Isles. While French settlers were overwhelmingly Catholic, Huguenots also made their way to the colonies; today it serves as the Centre d'interpretation de l'ardoise, or as it is more commonly known, the Slate Museum, but the church at the foot of Belmont Street, at the main intersection of what was once Lower Melbourne, was built as a Congregational Church before becoming L'Église St-Paul and serving a French Protestant congregation. American settlers—very many of whom were direct descendants of people who had come to the new world in search of religious freedom—were of several different Christian faiths: Presbyterian, Methodist, Congregationalist, among others. The very first places of worship were homes or multi-function buildings, a good example being the Stone Schoolhouse at Pierce's Crossing that was used for church services on Sundays and served as a school the rest of the week. A preacher would travel from one hamlet to the next, ministering to those of his faith and frequently to those of other faiths as well.

By 1838, four decades after Elmore Cushing had erected his mills on the small brook that spills into the St. Francis, the population had grown. There were hamlets on both sides of the river; not two, as the amalgamation of Melbourne and Richmond in 1999 would suggest, but four. On the west bank of the St. Francis were Upper Melbourne and Lower Melbourne, their two town halls little more than a kilometre apart. On the east bank of the river was Richmond East, and a kilometre upstream, the beginnings of what would be known, after the railway came through in 1855, as Richmond Station. The surrounding hinterland was increasingly dotted with homesteaders.

The second church to be erected in what was to become Richmond opened its doors in 1836. St. Bibiane's was a Catholic church. Today, not unlike most Catholic churches to be found in most towns and villages in rural Quebec, St. Bibiane's is a rather imposing brick structure. The church that was erected in 1836 was a modest wood-framed building that stood where the present church stands today, on a small bluff overlooking the St. Francis little more than a hundred yards away. (The site was far more bucolic at the time; today a criss-cross of bridge and rail yards blocks all views of the river.) The church was a mile or so downriver from Cushing's Brook.

Across the river, in Upper Melbourne, the same year, the St. Andrew's Presbyterian congregation—as yet without a place of worship of their own—engaged the Reverend Thomas MacPherson as their first minister. He is listed as the first of twenty-eight ministers who served St. Andrew's over a period of one hundred and seventy-five years; the last was the Reverend Mark Godin, who resigned his post in 2005, leaving the congregation to be served by lay preachers and occasional clergymen. It is not known why MacPherson stayed in Upper Melbourne just the one year (or some part of it), but the second minister to serve the Presbyterian faithful was John McMorine who arrived in 1839 and remained until 1846. It was under his watch that St. Andrew's Church was erected, as well as the Manse, which is now the home of the Richmond County Historical Society.

One of the driving forces behind the construction of the Presbyterian Church—one of the first to be built in the Eastern Townships—was Daniel Thomas. In 1841 he donated two pieces of land to the congregation: one, at the top of a long hill, became the site of St. Andrew's Cemetery; the other, near the bottom of the same hill, on a small escarpment much closer to the river, was where St. Andrew's Church and the Manse were built. (Daniel Thomas's own property was near the top of the hill, a few hundred metres below the cemetery.) The church was finished in 1842 and the Manse was in all likelihood completed shortly after.

During the same time that Thomas was working towards creating a suitable place of worship for the spiritual well-being of the local Presbyterians, he was also thinking of ameliorating their lives in another important way.

Given that the St. Francis was the first highway into Shipton and several other townships, it was understandable that small homesteads would be built on or near both banks of the river, and that hamlets would spring up on both banks. But it was just as normal that people would want to get from one side of the river to the other. From the time of Cushing's arrival, in 1798, until 1847, getting from Richmond to Melbourne required either swimming across, or crossing over on a small scow which provided ferry service. The scow, carrying both people and livestock, was poled across the relatively shallow river by a ferryman who charged for his labour.

It worked, but the scow could only carry so many passengers or goods at any one time; it took several minutes to get across; if the ferry were on the other bank a traveller might have a bit of a wait before it came to fetch him. At times the crossing could be more hazardous, as when the river was high and faster flowing; at other times, as when ice was forming in the late fall, and breaking up in the early spring, the ferryman might not want to cross at all.

What Thomas (and everyone else) wanted was a bridge. Even if it were a toll bridge, it would be faster and more dependable than crossing the river in a flat-bottomed barge. Cost was clearly a concern—could such a small place afford the expense of constructing a bridge? But even greater was the worry about durability. Could a bridge be built to withstand spring thaw, which almost always was accompanied by extensive flooding and floating ice pans, at times the size of a shed. What good is a bridge if it's going to be swept away by ice or high water every spring?

Thomas was a notary by training, but in a pioneer community where ingenuity and resourcefulness were necessary commodities, he also seems to have been something of an engineer by vocation. The bridge he designed was never built; nevertheless, it's interesting to note that this was not for lack of trying. The *Annals* quotes an address he would have delivered to government officials in Quebec City.

"For ten years I have concentrated my efforts towards the invention of a simple and effective means for the erection of a temporary bridge—one which could be taken apart—to preserve it from floods and ice—and I have succeeded in making a plan for a floating bridge which permits not only facility of communication at this point but would be a great public benefit in many other places in N. A. [North America] where floods and ice are destructive.

"This bridge would consist of two long rafts constructed on each bank—one end to be attached to the bank, the other pushed to the middle of the river to meet the raft from the opposite side and to form with it an acute angle, the whole fastened with chains and cables. I ask you to grant me the exclusive right to construct such bridges in Melbourne and the whole of Lower Canada. I beg you therefore to approve my company, The Richmond Floating Bridge Company."

As far as is known, the company was never formed and no actual attempt was ever made to construct the floating bridge. However, it's interesting to note that when a wood-framed, covered bridge was built to connect the communities on opposite banks in 1847, spring ice promptly took out a part of it early in 1848. The bridge was repaired and was used for the next thirty-two years, when a new bridge built of steel girders was erected to replace it in 1882. This new bridge was a source of controversy, as users had to pay a toll to use it, and many continued to use the wooden bridge even though it had been deemed dangerous. Eventually, the wooden bridge was destroyed by dynamite. The steel bridge of 1882 lasted a mere five years before spring ice tore out two of its five spans. It was repaired, but ice eventually carried it all away in 1901.

For his part, Thomas lived to see and use the wooden bridge, for several years. It's easy to imagine him saying, "I told you so," to whomsoever would listen in the spring of 1848.

Daniel Thomas died in 1856 at the age of sixty-five.

St. Francis River, circa 1920. This photo was likely taken south of Richmond, somewhere between Greenlay and Upper Melbourne, looking downriver. Only in rare places does the St. Francis not now have a wide riparian strip. (RCHS Archival Collection)

# CHAPTER 8

# Craig's Road

IN RICHMOND, Craig Street starts at the St. Francis River, at the east bank abutment of the MacKenzie Bridge. It crosses *rue Principale* and *rue du Collège* before curving gently uphill, over the viaduct and as far as the intersection of highway 143, where it becomes Highway 116 leading to Danville, and eventually to the south bank of the St. Lawrence River where it intersects Highway 132, that runs into Lévis. Travelling by car, as we all do today, from Richmond on the St. Francis to Lévis on the St. Lawrence via the 116 is a journey of one hundred and fifty-seven kilometres or ninety-four miles. Along the way, street names like *le chemin Craig,* or *la rue Craig* appear in half a dozen towns and villages: Danville, Tingwick, Ste-Hélène-de-Chester, and Saint-Patrice de Beaurivage, among others.

Highway 116 runs from the south shore of Montreal to Lévis, across the river from Quebec City. The eastern section of this highway follows a road first built more than two centuries ago on the instructions of General James Craig, who, from 1807 to 1811, was the controversial Governor of the two Canadas, and Lieutenant-Governor of Lower Canada; hence the frequent occurrence of streets and roads bearing Craig's name.

The Craig Road was cut through virgin forest from British North America's capital—Quebec City—to Shipton, little more than a decade after Elmore Cushing dragged his canoes onto the banks of the St. Francis. Curiously, it was both a primitive roadway to an isolated, nascent settlement and one leg of the land route of choice between Quebec City and Boston. This seeming contradiction stems from the fact that for eight or nine months of the year, the simplest way to travel or to ship goods from Boston to Quebec was by sail. During the winter months, with the St. Lawrence frozen solid, commerce came to a virtual standstill. The Craig Road, representing the northernmost quarter of the six-hundred-kilometre trek from the prosperous American seaport to the bastion of British North America, became, in 1811, the only alternative to bushwhacking through dense forest or snowshoeing up frozen rivers.

The Eastern Townships had been laid out not unlike English counties, and given names to reinforce the image of rural Britain: Dorchester, Leeds, Tingwick. Colonial administrators reasoned that such details would make the Townships that much more enticing to British immigrants. However, Americans had been the first to settle in this newly opened wilderness. No doubt all pledged fealty to King George III, but these same American settlers—or their parents—had only just rebelled against the same King George a scant generation before. What General James Craig really wanted was a large influx of Britons to insure that the colony would remain loyal. Settlers from the United Kingdom would also do much to promote the anglicization of Lower Canada, which was overwhelmingly French-speaking, even if English was unquestionably the language of governance and commerce.

While the Governor wanted a road built into the Townships, the Legislative Assembly, an elected body which, at least in theory, existed to advise and counsel the Governor General, was very set against it. Members of the Assembly were overwhelmingly French-speaking. English-speaking settlers were the last thing that the vast majority of the population of Lower Canada and their elected representatives wanted. Craig, whose duty was to his sovereign, and certainly not to the Roman-Catholic, French-speaking majority whose ancestors hailed from France, put aside the wishes of his elected advisors. It should also be remembered that the Napoleonic wars were raging and the British authorities were suspicious of the French-speaking *Canadiens.*

Although built by Craig in 1810, the road had been envisaged much earlier. In 1800, Joseph Kilborne, Lower Canada's Deputy Surveyor, undertook to trace a road from Quebec City into the Townships. According to John Hayes, a second surveyor (by coincidence named James Craig) "made a further opening, as far as the River St. Francis." It's easy to imagine that, even just a year or two after Elmore Cushing's arrival, a rough path would have already existed between the Front and Back Villages of Shipton. By 1810, when Craig undertook the construction of his road, that track would have become a primitive but useable roadway for people travelling on foot, or with a team of oxen or horses pulling a cart or wagon.

Among his papers, Dr. John Hayes, whose story is told in chapters 15 and 16, had a newspaper clipping that reads, in part:

Seventy-five miles of road was cut through the primeval forest in 1810 by four hundred regular soldiers of the Quebec Garrison, under the command of Lieut.-Col Robertson, when a first class carriage road was completed from Quebec to the village of Shipton, now known as Richmond, Que. The thoroughfare through the forest, which as yet for the most part was uninhabited, was generally fifteen feet wide, free from all stumps and other embarrassments, and consisted of no less than one hundred and twenty bridges of different dimensions. Of these, twenty-four spanned large streams and the Craig Bridge—named in honor of Sir James Craig, Governor of Canada from 1807 to 1811—built over the Bécancour River, was said to be of excellent workmanship. Of the hundred of troops engaged in the undertaking, not a single man died of disease or deserted. On their return in October of the above year, the officers and men composing the working force received the thanks of the military authorities for their splendid work. It was considered the most important undertaking since the conquest in 1759, as the free and easy access to such a beautiful and fertile country as the Eastern Townships would provide the necessary supplies for a growing population such as Quebec was having at that period in the city's history.

There is much that is remarkable about this passage. For one thing, since the distance from Lévis (across the St. Lawrence from Quebec City) to Richmond is ninety-four miles; how can seventy-five miles of roadway be sufficient to connect them? The answer is that Craig's soldiers started the new road at St. Nicolas, a few miles south west of Lévis, and, more significantly, their services were not needed for the last dozen miles, to the Front Village of Shipton on the St. Francis. After a decade of use, the roadway between the Front and Back Villages of Shipton would have been a step up from a rutted set of tracks through the forest, with a number of less travelled paths branching off to the homesteads of settlers such as Avery Denison. In all probability, the last twelve miles of the Craig Road to the St. Francis were the most easily travelled.

As confusing is the size of the contingent that embarked on the construction. Was it four hundred soldiers, as the newspaper article proclaims in the opening line, or was it one hundred as is indicated later in the same paragraph?

The assertion that what the soldiers built was a "first class carriage road" was more wishful thinking than fact. Today, no civil engineer with a hundred men (or even four hundred) would undertake to construct seventy-five miles of roadway in just a few months. Craig's troops set out in July of 1810 and returned in October of the same year. That men equipped with axes and saws and picks and shovels could build a road in three or four months speaks to the rough and improvised nature of the roadway built. The Craig Road was built quickly, but it needed repairs from the very beginning, and seems to have gone on needing repairs for most of the last two centuries.

Hayes notes that, "On Tuesday, July 13, 1811, working parties from the different regiments in the garrison at Quebec, to the number of about two hundred officers and men, again left Quebec, this time to open a road from St. Giles through the township of Leeds, Inverness, Halifax, Chester and Tingwick to Shipton on the St. Francis." The military work crew of 1811 was sufficiently large to suggest that the road was undergoing reconstruction as much as repairs.

Yet, even with two consecutive summers of construction work, the road seems to have fallen short of expectations. Hayes refers to a letter signed by "A Poor Farmer" dated at Shipton, December 4, 1811 and published in the *Quebec Gazette* of January 2, 1812. Hayes writes, "The writer complained that in the township of his district there were two thousand children living without baptism, upwards of six hundred men and women living together without lawful marriage and that the greatest number of their people had not, for ten years heard the word of God on the Sabbath day. As for the dead, they were disposed of in the same manner that most people dispose of a favourite dog that dies, by placing the body under a tree. The people were also without doctors. It was all due, the writer said, to the lack of roads."

The poor farmer's complaint is perhaps no less an exaggeration than the first class carriage road; it is also in marked contrast to the triumphant tone of an article from the same *Gazette* published a year earlier in November of 1810: "Craig's Road leads to richer lands and each forward mile means greater opportunities! Many hundred heads of cattle have already reached here by this road, to the consternation of the small but avid dealers of cattle and sheep, who, at times, have kept us in a state of famine. We do not hesitate to call this work the most important local event since this province became British."

Equally intriguing is the notice printed in the *Quebec Gazette* of December 31, 1810: "Public notice is given that a regular stage coach, Quebec to Boston, via Craig's Road will begin next January 10, 1811 and will be continued regularly (in the winter only). Coaches will leave Quebec and Boston on Mondays of each week, will meet at Stanstead on Wednesdays, and arrive at Quebec and Boston on Saturdays of the same week."

While the term 'stage coach' brings to mind a closed, horse-pulled carriage mounted on four big wheels, the Quebec to Boston stage, in the winter, would have had to have been a carriage mounted on runners. Even at that, the six-day trip must have been an adventure, and not without its hazards and delays. The *Quebec Gazette*, on March 28, 1811, reported: "The stage from Boston, due Saturday, arrived Tuesday night. It was delayed by bad roads due to the sudden and unusual arrival of spring weather at its southern end. From Boston to about seventy miles from Quebec the snow has almost melted, frost is coming out of the ground, rivers are at flood, brooks and low lands are flooded, and the road through wooded sections is encumbered by fallen trees."

It's worth noting as well that, while Craig's troops built an impressive one hundred and twenty bridges in 1810, there was still no bridge crossing the St. Francis River at Shipton. As long as the river remained frozen, the stage could cross on an ice bridge. The stage that made it to Quebec City three days late in March of 1811 must have managed to cross a still frozen river, even if smaller streams and rivers further south were running and flooding.

Was Craig's Road seen as an asset or a liability during the War of 1812-1814? The question remains moot. But immediately after the War, in 1814, the Government accepted requests for improvements and awarded a contract to repair twenty miles of road eastward from the St. Francis River at a cost of forty-five pounds per mile. Three years later, in 1817, British soldiers were again put to work on Craig's Road, this time with the task of widening the road from fifteen feet to eighteen and digging three-foot wide ditches on either side. Despite this amelioration, in 1818 a complaint was made that "Craig's road has twenty-three miles uncompleted." A decade later, in 1828, Craig's Road was so bad that a petition was presented to the government requesting that a Commissioner be appointed to restore and complete the road.

Joseph Bouchette (1774-1841) was a surveyor, militia officer, and the cartographer responsible for the first large-scale map of Lower Canada. Writing in 1834, he stated: "As the road is to be ditched for thirty miles and as fourteen bridges each about twenty feet long and three bridges above eighty feet long, besides causeways, are to be erected, two thousand pounds at least will be necessary to make the thirty miles a passable carriage road and as the road from the Township of Ireland to Mrs. Stocking's, a distance of thirty miles would require at least one thousand pounds more, it will be seen that the complete Craig's Road to Shipton would require at least three thousand pounds."

It's not easy to reconcile Bouchette's description, including the need to erect almost twenty bridges, to build a "passable" carriage road a distance of thirty miles to get to Shipton, with the "first class" carriage road that was so triumphantly celebrated as completed a quarter century before.

It's worth remembering just how few roads there were in the early 1800s. Hayes again:

> The main and only roads leading from the heart of these townships to the older settlements were: (1) "Craig's Road" which forms its intersection of the St. Francis in Shipton was opened to the settlements of St. Giles; (2) the "East and West River Roads" on the

St. Francis River, leading from Sherbrooke to the Baie St. Antoine on Lake St. Peter; (3) the road through Hatley, Stanstead, Bolton, Sutton, St. Armand's, Dunham and Stanbridge to the settlements of the Richelieu River had previously opened several entries to the State of Vermont with which constant intercourse was kept up. Craig's Road was very little frequented on account of the obstacles with numerous swamps and wind falls threw on the way of travellers, particularly between Leeds and Shipton.

Hayes continues:

Of the roads along the St. Francis, that on the eastern bank was best and most generally used in summer; the other was used preferably in winter. The worst part of the summer road was between Courval and Spicers—six miles—of these four were called the savanne which in the wet season was dangerous and frequently impracticable. The bogs in the southern quarter of Simpson were another impediment to the traveller's progress for about half a league, but it was ascertained not to be perilous from the firmness of the substratum of the swamp. Of the last road that part traversing Potton and Sutton was the most rugged, broken and bad. The minor public roads, connecting the settlements of the Townships circumjacent to Ascot were numerous and generally much better, having the advantage of receiving more frequent repairs from the settlers to be found in greater numbers in this quarter of the tract than in any of the lands in Shipton.

Over time, Craig's Road became Highway 5 and eventually Highway 116. The road was straightened, moved, ditched, raised, gravelled, tarred, and paved in fits and starts as horses and carts gave way to cars and trucks. Through the nineteenth century and almost to the end of the twentieth, the road that James Craig ordered built remained a work in progress, a source of constant complaints and drain on the public purse. Ironically, the first stretch of road built—from Richmond to Danville—a stretch that pre-dates Craig, remained the roughest stretch of the entire road for the longest time. It wasn't until the 1980s that this piece of road was extensively redesigned and recast as an enjoyable stretch of highway to drive.

Today, taking Highway 116 from Richmond to Danville is a scenic and comfortable drive, and it is possible to continue on the 116 to Quebec City. However, as a route of choice to get from the Townships to Quebec City, the old Craig Road has been superseded by the four-lane *autoroutes*—the 55 and the 20 —that add kilometres to the trip but reduce the time it takes to make it.

CHAPTER 9

# *La Première Canadienne*

THE FIRST CANADIANS were *les Canadiens*, French-speaking North Americans. By the time the Eastern Townships were opened up for settlement in the last decade of the eighteenth century, *les Canadiens* had been populating the fertile river valley that links the Atlantic to the Great Lakes for close to two centuries. They had remained in the St. Lawrence Valley not so much because the alluvial soil was richer and more productive, but because the hilly, densely-wooded Townships provided at least partial protection from the Protestant English-speakers along the American seaboard to the south. They were also turned more to the West and the *pays d'en haut*, meaning the Great Lakes basin. Then, when the British authorities did open up the Townships for settlement, the intent was to attract English-speaking immigrants from the British Isles. Even though *les Canadiens* were as geographically close as the first American settlers (if not closer), they constituted the last wave of early settlers in the Townships.

The *Annals* make almost no mention at all of early French-speaking settlers, yet today it is French speakers who make up at least ninety percent of the population in the Richmond area (and ninety-five percent of the Eastern Townships). Such a demographic shift occurs over decades or even centuries, but inevitably must begin with one individual or a small group. Who, then, was the first *Canadien* to establish himself in Richmond or its hinterland?

The only answer so far comes from Joseph-Charles St-Amant (1859–1939). A notary who lived most of his life in L'Avenir (eighteen kilometres north of Richmond), St-Amant was a dynamic individual who was very involved with his community. In 1898 he published a book entitled *L'Avenir et ses environs*, which was re-published in 1932 under the title *Un coin des Cantons de l'Est.*

From St-Amant's perspective, L'Avenir is "*la première colonie organisée du premier coin enfoncé dans…la Province des Cantons de l'Est.*" (Later he will refer to *les Townships de l'Est* and *la Province des Townships du Sud.*) The image evoked by St-Amant of a sharp corner being sunk into a body is somewhat cartographic—the Townships having been laid out as big squares; on a map, Wickham Township is indeed delineated by a right angle that pokes into what he calls the Province of the Eastern Townships. On nineteenth century maps, Wickham does resemble an obstinate square falling corner-first into a quilt of quadrilaterals.

And while St-Amant states clearly that his adopted village is the first colony in the Eastern Townships, his readers must understand that L'Avenir was the first settlement made up primarily (if not entirely) of *Canadiens* (as opposed to settlers of British stock). St-Amant is clearly aware that, when L'Avenir's first settlers started putting down roots, the two settlements that would eventually become Richmond and Sherbrooke were already well established further up river, as were dozens of other English-speaking settlements. St-Amant describes the founder of Drummondville, Frederick George Heriot, as wanting to reach Richmond or Sherbrooke but, finding himself blocked by waterfalls, opting instead to establish a military camp on the site of Drummondville.

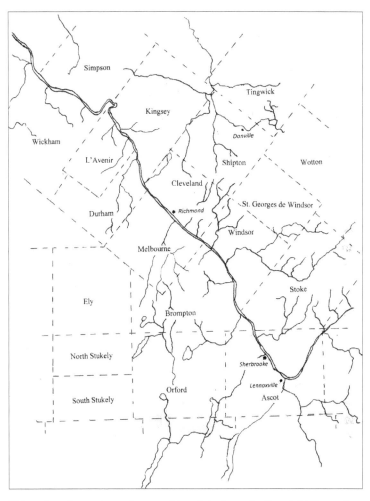

This artisanal map shows the townships of the lower St. Francis Valley as they would have appeared at the time of Confederation. Note that Shipton has already been subdivided into Shipton and Cleveland.

St-Amant states, *"Jusque vers 1840 la colonisation des Cantons de l'Est par les Canadiens-Français marcha à pas lents."*

He goes on, *"Il fallait une forte dose de courage pour affronter les misères de toute sorte occasionnées par la pauvreté d'abord et par l'antipathie de la population anglo-saxonne et celtique."*

If there was bad blood between *les premiers colons* and the Anglo-Saxons and Celts as St-Amant says, there was also love. Fittingly, it was the latter that led the first *Canadienne*, to venture into Richmond County.

"The first representative of our race in the Township of Wickham and of Durham," St-Amant writes, "was a woman, widow of a Canadian dragoon killed in 1812 and wed in a second marriage to one of the soldiers of the Meurons regiment, I believe: Mrs. Marie-Anne Blais, widow of Augustin Moisan and wife of Henry Wright."

Henry Wright was one of Major Frederick George Heriot's (1786–1844) disbanded soldiers who opted to accept an offer of land in the Eastern Townships. Following the war of 1812-1814, the British administration saw an opportune way to solve two problems with one deft move. The two problems were how to populate the distant Eastern Townships with Britons and what to do in England with a returning influx of soldiers. The solution was straightforward and simple: veterans of the war were offered land in the Townships. In the case of Heriot's troops, these included men who came from England and Ireland, but also German mercenaries, as well as *des Canadiens* and Abenaki militiamen.

Heriot, who was not yet thirty when the war ended, resigned from the army and took an administrative post through which he established Drummondville in 1815. He laid out plans for the settlement, established two missions—Anglican and Catholic—attracted many disbanded soldiers to the area, and ably administered the settlement until his death at age fifty-eight. Rather exceptionally, his name was given both to the Anglican church, St. George's, and to the Catholic church, *Saint-Frédéric*, in Drummondville.

Henry Wright was granted a plot of land in Wickham Township in 1815, but moved a little deeper inland, into Durham Township, very likely within the next year or two. (On the west side of the St. Francis, Durham Township borders on Melbourne Township and includes the village of Ulverton.) A great many of Wright's comrades in arms did likewise. Both time and place dealt harshly with those soldiers turned farmers. The year Heriot and Wright and many others started putting roots down in the Townships, was the year that Tambora erupted in the south Pacific Ocean, putting up such a cloud of volcanic dust that 1816 was recorded in the northern hemisphere as the year there was no summer. It wasn't a year to start farming. Nor was the place ideal; the flatlands around Drummondville are the sandy bottom of an ancient inland sea, for farmers not nearly as rich a soil as the loam found further upstream towards Richmond and Sherbrooke.

If Marie-Anne Blais was the first *Canadienne* to reside in the Richmond area, she may have been linguistically lonely but, assuming she was Catholic, she was not entirely without spiritual sustenance.

St-Amant paints the following picture: "While wealthy Anglophilic speculators, the "associates" of the Township of Durham, sought to preserve the Anglo-Saxon preponderance in our Township, a few "oases" opened up here and there, one could see, from time to time, a new plume of smoke rising at different places above the deep forests of maple and hemlock; no road linked these isolated centres, and yet one could feel that a magical force, invisible yet real, linked them together.

"The inhabitants of these impoverished cabins knelt morning and evening to raise towards the sky an ardent prayer and from time to time a man wearing a black robe arriving through the forest, came to visit them."

St-Amant notes that the first missionary to serve Heriot's nascent colony was Jean Raimbault who served his first mass on the feast of Corpus Christi in 1815. (We no longer follow a liturgical calendar, but Corpus Christi is a moveable holy day that falls sixty days after Easter.) Raimbault remained in the area and, as St-Amant points out, he laid the first stone for the church in St. Félix-de-Kingsey in 1835.

Raimbault was joined in his mission in 1823 by John Holmes. Holmes was born Protestant in the United States, but converted to Catholicism. He served an area that seems to us today inconceivably vast: his mission stretched from Drummondville all the way to Stanstead on the American border. Today, on a fast-flowing divided highway, the trip takes an hour and twenty minutes; for Holmes, travelling on foot, it's hard to imagine the walk taking less than three days.

Holmes undoubtedly followed a circuit that would have brought him to multiple places, even if these were no more than a string of isolated cabins. His congregation was not only widely spread but also diverse. He would have tended to the *Canadiens*, like Marie-Anne Blais, but also to English-speaking Catholics, some of whom would have been fellow-immigrants from the United States, as well as those from the United Kingdom and Ireland.

It's interesting to note that of the four priests who served this far-flung mission between 1815 and 1853, only Raimbault was French-speaking by birth. The Catholic Church appointed English-speaking priests to the area because, even among Catholics, English was the predominant language during those early years. However, by the middle of the nineteenth century, the demographic shift from English-speaking to French-speaking was already so well established that the parishes that were carved out of that huge original mission were predominantly French from the start.

Holmes has a slight but particular connection to the Richmond area. Holmes began purchasing small tracts of land on his far-flung circuit, foreseeing the time when growing populations would warrant the building of churches. In Shipton, he purchased a piece of land on Brandt's Hill, a rise of land roughly halfway between what is now Richmond and Danville. He consecrated the small mission church that was built there in 1829. Several years later, it burned down and a new church was built, not there but in Richmond, on a rise of land overlooking the river, where St. Bibiane's still stands today.

The first *Canadienne* to settle in the Richmond area then was Marie-Anne Blais. Parish records at St. Bibiane's begin in 1850. Records from Richmond prior to this date were kept in Drummondville and have since been transcribed and transferred to the Drummondville Genealogy Society. While names and dates are readily found, there is no easy way to associate the names with particular areas. The first *Canadien* or *Canadienne* to settle in Richmond proper remains unknown.

CHAPTER 10

# Annance and the Disappearance
# of the Abenaki

THERE ARE AXIOMS IN FIELDS other than mathematics and one is that history is written by the victors. The history of Richmond County is replete with stories about the hardships overcome by the early settlers from Vermont, Ireland, England, and Wales, about felling forests, eking out a living from subsistence farms, building roads and later railways, and about the growth of villages and towns to accommodate a rapidly growing population.

There is little said about the people who lived in the St. Francis River Valley between the time that glaciers retreated north and the time that Elmore Cushing paddled south to settle in Shipton. Yet, the Townships had been inhabited for at least part of the ten thousand years before 1798. What became of those people?

Through most of the Americas, indigenous peoples suffered unspeakable horrors under newly-arrived Europeans (the ramifications of which remain to this day). Save for the Inuit and the Patagonians, who inhabited climates too inhospitable to merit exploration and invasion in the sixteenth and seventeenth centuries, Native Americans were dispossessed, enslaved, massacred, and, in some cases, driven to extinction. It's only by comparison that the slow and almost total disappearance and assimilation of the Abenaki attracts little notice.

The Abenaki found themselves in the Townships in the eighteenth century in part because the wars between France and England had spilled over the Atlantic to the eastern shore of North America. For who knows how long, the Abenaki had lived along the seaboard of what are now the New England States. Pushed west by the Pilgrims in the early sixteen hundreds, the Abenaki were taken as allies by the French, and they moved into what is now the Eastern Townships and Vermont. In so doing, the Abenaki forced out the Iroquois who, in their turn, pushed west.

Not that the relationship of the Abenaki to the land was anything like that of the new arrivals. For the most part, the people who lived in the temperate zones of eastern North America were semi-nomadic people who were both hunter-gatherers and farmers. Open land used to grow corn, beans, and squash during the summer months was communal land, not privately owned. Everyone fished equally from the rivers. Just as no man held title to his own forty acres, there were no borders or customs officers demarcating one nation from another. Family clans would spend the winter months in relative isolation, living as best they could on dried corn and whatever fresh meat the forest might provide. In the summer the clans would come together at places like Three Forks—which became Hyatt's Mills, and then Sherbrooke—to erect summer quarters.

Once the Townships were surveyed and opened to settlers like Cushing and Denison, the way of life of the Abenaki changed quickly and irrevocably. A family of hunter-gatherers needs far more land to sustain itself than a family of farmers and herders. In terms of numbers, it's certain that by the second half of the nineteenth century, the Abenaki population was a small minority centred at Odanak, at the mouth of the St. Francis, and at Wôlinak, at the mouth of the Bécancour River.

St-Amant notes that, of the nine thousand acres of land granted by Heriot to Abenaki soldiers following the war of 1812-1814, almost all had reverted to white settlers two decades later. By 1833, only half a dozen Abenaki families were still farming in the lower St. Francis Valley.

Traces of assimilation by way of intermarriage still remain. Two centuries after Cushing's arrival, there are a number of Townshippers who claim, with increasing pride, that they carry Abenaki blood, traced back to a great, or great-great-grandparent.

Where did the Abenaki go?

One young Abenaki man went West.

There are few biographies, however brief, of Native Americans of the eighteenth and nineteenth centuries. Morag Maclachlan, writing in *The Beaver* (which has since become *Canada's History Magazine*) in 1993, painted a rather sympathetic portrait of Francis Noël Annance.

Genetically, Annance was not fully Abenaki, although his roots were so unusual they bear mentioning. His maternal great-grandparents were Samuel Gill and Rosalie James who were both born in Massachusetts to English families, but were abducted during the course of an Abenaki raid. They were brought back to Odanak, adopted by Abenaki families and, in turn, they adopted the Abenaki way of life. In 1715, they married and had five sons and two daughters. The Gill name, for the next four or five generations, continued to be linked to the Odanak area. Through the eighteenth and nineteenth centuries, and into the twentieth, sons, great-grandsons, and great-great-grandsons of Samuel Gill and Rosalie James took on leadership roles: Chief of the Abenaki, Member of the National Assembly, Judge of the Superior Court, painter and poet.

Francis Noël Annance was born in 1789. As had three generations of ancestors before him, Annance grew up in the area around Odanak, but received a few years of education at Moor's Indian Charity School in Hanover, New Hampshire, which later became Dartmouth College. During the war of 1812, he was made a lieutenant under the command of Sir John Johnson. He then became a schoolmaster but, in 1819, he joined the North West Company and journeyed to the Pacific coast to work as a trapper, earning fifty pounds a year plus a percentage of the profits on the furs he harvested.

Only three years later, the North West Company was absorbed by the Hudson Bay's Company (HBC). While a number of trappers suddenly found themselves unemployed, Annance was hired by the new firm which seemed to appreciate him, though not necessarily in the manner Annance would have wished. On one of the expeditions for which he was chosen, he kept a journal that was later sent to Hudson Bay's headquarters and reflects his formal education—a knowledge of the classics and a more elaborate literary style. He felt that his education would provide him with opportunities for advancement.

It was not to be. Annance was considered more valuable for his skills as a woodsman and hunter, and was frequently sent on challenging expeditions. He was considered that much more valuable by HBC for having been educated in English, being fluent in French, and possessing a working knowledge of several Native languages.

By the time he was forty, he had begun to grow bitter. Annance had seen men he worked with given promotions that, in a just world, would have gone to him; he was literate, hard-working, and not without qualities of leadership. Yet, when he requested his early release from the fur trading company, it was refused. The only concession accorded by the HBC was to promote him to postmaster, the highest rank available to men of mixed-blood.

Ironically, just a few years later, the same company that refused to release him turned around and demanded his resignation, not for professional, but rather for personal reasons. Annance had been sent to Fort Simpson, on the MacKenzie River in the North West Territories, to work under John Stuart. Stuart's "country wife" (a woman accepted as his wife for all practical purposes, but not legally married to him) fell in love with Annance. When the affair was discovered, it rapidly led to the end of his career with the company.

Annance returned to the Odanak area in 1845 to resume his earlier job as a school teacher. It is likely that he did some farming along with his teaching. He is listed in the 1851 census as being married with two children, although this would have been a second marriage for him. He had three boys, one of whom drowned, from an earlier marriage with a Native woman in the West.

In 1867, Annance was one of the witnesses at the Connolly-Woolrich trial, which determined that "country marriages" were legally binding—a legal precedent that cleared the way for common-law marriages that began proliferating a century later. Francis Noël Annance. died two years later, in 1869, and was buried in the Cross Cemetery which was once found near the confluence of the Ulverton and St. Francis Rivers.

# PART 3

# FROM RIVER TO RAIL, MID-CENTURY TO THE GREAT WAR

The 5060. Taken near the intersection of King and Main Street,
likely in the late 1940s, this photo captures Canadian National's steam
locomotive, 5060, possibly coming back from the roundhouse
where repairs and maintenance were carried out.
(RCHS, McCarthy Collection)

# CHAPTER 11

# Richmond and the Railway

THE FIRST EUROPEAN SETTLERS came to the northern part of the Eastern Townships by—and because of—the river. Half a century later, some of the villages that had slowly taken root on the river banks grew into towns when they might, almost as easily, have withered into little more than crossroads. Richmond in particular benefited from the invention and development of the steam locomotive that, in the second half of the nineteenth century, revolutionized transportation.

The idea of using rails to minimize friction was already old when George Stephenson combined rails with steam engines to create the world's first railway in 1825. Horses had been used to haul wagons and carriages along rails since Roman times, if not earlier. Stone and timber had both been used to facilitate hauling heavy loads before steel rails, similar to those used today, were first tried early in the 1600s. Stephenson's first railway was about forty kilometres long and connected two relatively unknown places, Darlington and Stockton, in the northeast of England. The former was near coal fields and the latter was on a river giving access to the North Sea. Five years later, in 1830, Stephenson built the first public inter-city railway from Manchester to Liverpool.

It was the beginning of the end of the horse-drawn wagon. Stephenson proved that steam trains were economically more viable than horses. A steam train could haul more tonnage and get from one point to another faster than any team of horses. The initial investment required for a rail line might be very high, but the long-term benefits were incontestable. Not just in England, but on all continents except Antarctica, men with money and imagination set out to build railways.

Richmond's history has been closely linked to the railway since several years before 1851, when the first steam train chugged its way from Montreal to the east bank of the St. Francis River. At least part of that history is as nebulous as the clouds of steam that were puffed out of those nineteenth century boilers. Why, for example, did the tracks run to Richmond when common sense would have dictated that they go to Melbourne?

The rail tracks that reached Richmond from Montreal in 1851 represented part of the Canadian leg of the St. Lawrence & Atlantic line linking Montreal to Portland, Maine. As an ice-free port, Portland was open year-round. A rail line linking Montreal to Portland meant that goods and people could move between the Canadian colonies and mother England at all times of the year.

In retrospect, Portland might seem an odd choice for a rail terminal. Why not Boston, or New York, both much more economically viable cities? Part of the answer is that John Poor, a lawyer and journalist, and native of Bangor, Maine, lobbied actively for a Montreal-Portland line. He was successful enough that, in the winter of 1843, a race was organized to determine which of two proposed rail routes might be faster. A steamer from England docked at Portland and unloaded half the Montreal-bound mail it was carrying. A day or two later, it unloaded the rest of the Montreal mail in Boston. In each case the mail was put on a dog sled and the two teams set off through the wilderness and up frozen rivers heading for Montreal along the two proposed rail routes. The Boston sled took twelve hours longer to complete its trip and Portland got the rail terminal.

The railway company that was formed to build the line was known as the Atlantic & St. Lawrence Railway in the United States but was called the St. Lawrence & Atlantic Railway in Canada. Construction started simultaneously at the extremities of the line with crews laying track towards the east or north as the case might be. The last stretch of track to be laid was the seventy kilometres between Sherbrooke and Island Pond, Vermont. It was 1853 before the first train was able to make it from Montreal to Portland.

Donald Healy is a descendant of one of the area's very early settlers, and a past-president of the Richmond County Historical Society.

"I haven't done the research on this, so I can't say exactly who was involved and what kind of deals were struck," he says, "but there must have been some political strings pulled, and pulled quite hard, because it's not Richmond, but Melbourne, on the west bank of the St. Francis, that should have had a railway station. Running the tracks to Richmond necessitated the building of two bridges, the first one just downriver from Richmond to get to the east bank, and the second just downriver from Sherbrooke to get back to the west bank. Two railway trestle bridges represented a lot of expense. Why cross the same river twice when you don't have to cross it at all?"

The answer may lay in the fact that in 1854 or 1855 (dates vary according to sources) a second railway line, running from Richmond to Lévis, was started.

In the 1840s, when the railways were being plotted out on the map, Quebec City was the political and financial hub of the two Canadas. If it made sense to run a line to Montreal, the gateway to rapidly expanding Upper Canada, it was equally important to link Quebec City and its hinterland to an ice-free port. Considering the political clout that comes of being a colonial capital, it becomes easier to imagine that the power brokers in Quebec City might have had considerable influence on locating a train station on the east side of the St. Francis, to the benefit of the Quebec-Richmond Railway.

The choice of Richmond was contrary to expectations. In the several years following the announcement of the Montreal-Portland line, there was considerable land speculation going on in Melbourne where landowners looked forward to selling swaths of land to the railroad. At the time, the two Melbournes, Upper and Lower, were larger and more prosperous than the villages across the river. There was every reason to believe that one of the two villages on the west bank would get a much coveted railroad stop.

Were the costs of building the two bridges too much for the St. Lawrence & Atlantic? Was the cost of the Quebec-Richmond line (even without a bridge over the St. Francis) equally burdensome? Whatever the case, in 1856 both the St. Lawrence & Atlantic and the Quebec-Richmond Railways became part of the Grand Trunk Railway (GTR) that would go on to become the biggest railway line in the world. (In the case of the Quebec-Richmond Railroad, it was purchased by the Grand Trunk even before the line was completed.)

"A fact that is not well-known," Healy explains, "is that Richmond's first railway station and yards were located almost a mile upstream from the site where they presently sit. This put the original station essentially at the foot of the first bridge, a place that for a long time was known as the wood-yard, in part because the early steam locomotives burned wood and a good supply had to be kept on hand; and in part because considerable quantities of lumber were being shipped by rail. That location, at the time, made considerable sense. Someone getting off the train would have had instant access to both sides of the river thanks to the bridge that had been built just a few years before. As well, Richmond originally had grown south of Cushing Brook, so that the station was close to the centre of the town as it existed then.

"Again," he continues, "I haven't done enough research to do more than speculate on this, but there were undoubtedly some political forces at work that led to the station and yards being moved downstream."

One factor, he suggests, may well have been the location of the Richmond end of the Quebec-Richmond line. It's not clear exactly when the station and yards were moved downstream, but it was very early on, possibly even within two or three years of the construction of the original station. This poses a chicken-and-egg type question. Was it the trajectory of the Quebec line that prompted the yards to be moved, or were plans already underway to move the yards when the Quebec line was laid? (The answer may be that the steep escarpment near the original rail yards posed a more difficult, and more costly, engineering challenge than moving the train station.)

The other factor Healy points to is that while the arrival of the railroad promised prosperity, it also brought with it more than a little inconvenience. Steam trains were loud and too easily able to spook horses. They spewed out not just clouds of smoke but also burning embers that posed a very real and substantial fire hazard to the shops and houses in the vicinity of the rail line as those early buildings generally had cedar shingle roofs that could catch fire all too quickly. Cedar, the same wood used for roofing shingles, is unsurpassed as kindling wood for starting fires.

"I suspect," Healy says, "that once they experienced the downside of living with a train station, Richmond's burghers were anxious to relocate the station and yards just a little further away.

"The GTR went to quite a bit of trouble," he continues, "because the new shunting yards and station were built on landfill, and this at a time long before heavy machinery, a time when everything was done by men with picks and shovels and horse-drawn wagons hauling sand and gravel."

If using landfill was a way to avoid buying land, it hardly seems a profitable financial trade-off. As Healy points out, reclaiming low-lying land along the river solved one problem at the expense of creating another.

"The St. Francis had always been prone to flooding, as it still is," he says. "By filling in what were most likely swamp and marshland, the GTR effectively made the river narrower. Constricting the flow of water would have only added to the flooding. The rail yards are several feet higher than most of Main Street, and only rarely have they ever been under water, but Main Street itself was flooded regularly until the construction of the dike in the mid-1980s."

The GTR operated between 1853 and 1923, when it and its subsidiaries were merged into the Canadian National Railway (CNR). The GTR made Richmond a rail hub and the CNR continued to use it as such until the late 1950s, when diesel locomotives started replacing steam engines. As a junction connecting Montreal and the West to both Portland and Quebec City (and eventually, in 1877, Halifax), Richmond would have been a place of note on the map.

The importance of that dot on the map was further enhanced in 1872 when the GTR decided to make Richmond the site of its maintenance and repair yards. A roundhouse was built with eighteen bays. A turntable allowed locomotives to be easily shunted into one or another of the bays where mechanics could work on the massive steam engines.

For more than half a century, the Richmond railway shops provided steady, well-paid employment to as many as four hundred men.

GTR Wreck at Richmond, August 31, 1904. A head-on collision between the
Montreal special excursion train en route to the Sherbrooke Exhibition and
No. 5, Island Pond, local passenger train en route to Montreal occurred
at the "Wood Yard" about a mile south of the GTR Station.
With nine dead and twenty-five injured, the accident was one
of the worst in the history of the Grand Trunk Railway.
(RCHS Archival Collection, *The Times and County Record*,
September 2, 1904.)

For a short period of time, there was a second railroad that
opened a line into the Richmond area, although not to
Richmond itself. The rise and fall of the Orford Mountain
Railway (OMR) is not untypical of railroad ventures of the time.
A great many were built, so much so that for a time the Eastern
Townships had a greater concentration of rail lines than any-
where else in Canada. However, although many were built,
almost as many failed to survive.

The OMR was granted a charter in 1888 to build a railroad from Eastman to Lawrenceville and elsewhere, including areas previously allotted to the Missisquoi & Black Rivers Valley Railway that had been granted a charter in 1870 to run from Mansonville, on the U.S. border, to Durham or Richmond. That rail line was never completed. Construction of the OMR got underway in 1891 and by 1894 the OMR was operating from Eastman to Kingsbury. Lumber and lumber by-products accounted for half of its tonnage and it operated profitably until 1906 when, as a direct result of constructing three new spurs, it began losing money.

In 1910, the Canadian Pacific Railway (CPR) took over the OMR through an Order-in-Council by which the OMR was leased to the CPR for nine hundred and ninety-nine years. Under the CPR, the OMR line was extended both to the north to Golden Bay on the St. Francis River and along its west bank to Greenlay, across the river from Windsor, and to the south to Troy Junction, just over the border in Vermont.

Only a few years after this expansion, in 1914, the OMR started contracting and one of its branch lines was torn up to be used elsewhere as part of the First World War effort. A second section of the track was abandoned in 1936, and in 1942 another section of the rail line was dismantled to provide scrap steel as part of the Second World War effort. Finally, in 1965, the last remaining tracks of the OMR were abandoned.

Fifty years after it was dismantled, there are still a few remaining vestiges of its relatively brief existence. It's still possible, by venturing in kayak or canoe into the Kingsbury marsh, to see the remains of a trestle bridge that was part of the OMR rail line.

In Richmond the railway has made a curious sort of revival. By the 1950s, truck transportation was starting to compete with rail freight. At the same time, passenger trains were losing the

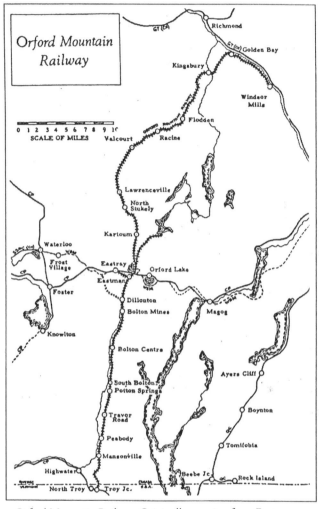

Orford Mountain Railway. Originally running from Eastman to
Kingsbury, the Orford Mountain Railway briefly ran from the U.S.
border to Greenlay, across the St. Francis from Windsor. Like many
other railways, it was short-lived and operated from 1892 until 1949.
(RCHS Archives, McKenzie Page collection.)

battle with the family sedan. CNR closed the roundhouse in Richmond in 1965, as the last of the steam locomotives were replaced by diesel engines. The last passenger train left the Richmond station in 1985 and the station itself was sold a few years later to two entrepreneurs, Gerry St. Laurent and Gerald Blom, who turned the building into a restaurant and a motel.

In 1998, CNR sold its tracks from Sainte-Rosalie in Quebec to Auburn, Maine, to a new company with an old name, the St. Lawrence & Atlantic. In the last two decades, it has grown slowly but steadily and has managed to make a profit where CNR was losing money. The few dozen employees now working on the railroad in Richmond can hardly match the four hundred who worked there seventy-five years ago, but they continue to keep Richmond on the railway map.

CHAPTER 12

# Ephrem Brisebois
# and the Mounted Police

T HE SMALL VILLAGE OF SOUTH DURHAM is not twinned with booming, oil-rich Calgary. Yet there would be at least one reason for the two very disparate places to be formally linked.

The man who founded Calgary as an RCMP outpost in 1875 was born in South Durham, and were it not for a particularly harsh prairie winter and an illicit love affair, Alberta's most prosperous city would likely be known today as Brisebois and not Calgary. As it is, Calgary has a major artery that bears his name.

Ephrem-A. Brisebois was born in 1850 in South Durham. (The unknowns regarding Brisebois begin with his name. *The Dictionary of Canadian Biography* refers to him as Ephrem-A., yet a photo from the 1870s identifies him as Ephrem-Albert. It is also possible that he was christened Ephrem-Amable as genealogical records indicate that Amable was his maternal grandfather's name.)

*The Dictionary of Canadian Biography* identifies Brisebois' father as a hotel keeper and a justice of the peace in Drummondville. Local records indicate that Brisebois *père* obtained a permit—at a cost of twenty dollars—to sell alcohol in South Durham in 1866.

Brisbois *fils* was raised in a devout Roman Catholic family that believed in education. He grew up fluently bilingual.

In 1865, aged fifteen, he quit school and went to the United States where he enlisted in the Union Army just before the American Civil War ended.

He returned to Quebec only to enlist in another army; this time the Zouaves, an international brigade of unmarried, young, Catholic men recruited by Pope Pius IX to protect the Papal States against the forces of Giuseppe Garibaldi who was fighting to unite Italy into a single, independent country. (Italy achieved unification in 1870, when Pius IX finally surrendered Rome.) Brisebois was part of a brigade, known as the Devils of the Good Lord, for the better part of three years before he returned to Canada.

In 1873, when the North-West Mounted Police (NWMP) was formed, Brisebois was appointed as one of its nine commanding officers by Prime Minister John A. MacDonald, and this despite the fact that Brisebois was only twenty-three years old. In spite of his young age, he was an experienced soldier and, perhaps just as important, he and his family were staunch Conservative supporters of MacDonad. He was the first French-Canadian officer of the force.

He helped recruit men for the NWMP and in the winter of 1873-1874 he marched his troops from Port Arthur (now Thunder Bay) to Lower Fort Garry (now a historic site just north of Winnipeg), a distance of over seven hundred kilometres. He spent the winter training his recruits and, in the summer of 1874, after being promoted to the rank of Inspector, he started a long march westward. One task given to the NWMP was to help open up the Canadian west for settlement, specifically by putting an end to the practices of American whiskey traders and establishing a climate of law and order. The Mounties were sent as well to assert Canadian/British sovereignty in the West. At the time, there were some in the U.S. who claimed that all the West should belong to the United States. The neophyte police force, despite its small size (approximately two hundred and seventy-five men; different sources give both smaller and larger numbers), was also expected to prevent the U.S. cavalry from moving into Canada.

Ironically, the Mounties swung through Montana before reaching southern Alberta. Brisebois helped erect Fort MacLeod, located less than one hundred kilometres from the American border, and named in honour of James MacLeod, Assistant Commissioner of the NWMP, and Brisebois' immediate superior.

Brisebois, seemingly after a disagreement with MacLeod, was sent with a small detachment to establish Fort Kipp, about forty kilometres distant.

In 1875, Brisebois led a troop of fifty men some two hundred kilometres north and, at the juncture of the Bow and Elbow Rivers, erected another palisaded encampment. In imitation of his nemesis, MacLeod, he named the place Fort Brisebois. The following winter was especially harsh and a few things transpired which eventually led to Brisebois quitting the force. It's probable that the key factor was that Brisebois fell in love with a young Métis woman who became his common-law wife, to the great chagrin of both Catholic and Protestant missionaries. Worse, this almost certainly aroused more than a little jealousy among his men. Perhaps because he was distracted by the Métis maiden, Brisebois became negligent in his duties. He let discipline slide. He allowed his men to use the weather as an excuse to avoid routine tasks. He failed to have cabins built for two interpreters at a nearby Métis camp. At a certain point, he appropriated the fort's only cook-stove to heat his own quarters.

He was sharply criticized by his superior officer who, in June of 1876, changed the name of Fort Brisebois to Fort Calgary.

Brisebois resigned from the NWMP and rode alone back to Winnipeg via Fort Edmonton. At age twenty-six, his career with the Mounties was over.

During his time with the force Brisebois seems to have been in fairly frequent conflict with his superior officer. James MacLeod was born on the Isle of Skye and grew up in Richmond Hill, Ontario. He attended Upper Canada College (still one of the country's most prestigious private schools) before going on to Queen's University and Osgoode Hall to study law. He was some fifteen years older than Brisebois and it's interesting to speculate why the two men did not get along with each other since both are described as being popular.

It's MacLeod who had the last word, at least as far as Calgary goes. MacLeod named Calgary after a small village in Scotland best known for its sandy beach. The MacLeod Trail, which is today one of Calgary's major thoroughfares, bears his name. One of his daughters married one of the founders of the Calgary Stampede and one of his granddaughters was one of the first women to be elected to Calgary's city council. Today, MacLeod—not Brisebois—is given credit as having founded the city.

For all his shortcomings, especially in the eyes of his superior officer, Brisebois showed some prescience. He was deeply concerned that the wanton slaughter of buffalo would lead to dire consequences. (It's worth mentioning that the original name of Regina, before it became Saskatchewan's capital, was Pile of Bones, the bones being those of buffalo.) He tried to enforce strict hunting regulations and, in 1875, warned that unless buffalo hunts were regulated the Amerindian population would be facing starvation within ten years. As it turned out, only five years later Native people started becoming dependent on the government for food.

From the West, Brisebois went to Ottawa where he failed to find work and so returned to Quebec and got involved in politics. In 1877, during a by-election in Drummond-Arthabaska, he campaigned assiduously for Désiré-Olivier Bourbeau, the Conservative candidate who defeated a future prime minister, Wilfrid Laurier.

In 1880, he returned to the Canadian West, this time as the land titles registrar for the Little Saskatchewan district in south-western Manitoba. He married the daughter of a retired British Army officer. (The bride's family name was Malcourrone but—depending on the source—her given name was Marie or Adelle.) The couple settled in Minnedosa, Manitoba, about two hundred kilometres west of Winnipeg. The Catholic population of the town was so small that church services were held in their home; the Brisebois were socially active and were the founders of the local snowshoe club.

During the North-West rebellion of 1885 (also known as the Second Riel Rebellion), Brisebois organized two companies of white and Métis home guards to prevent bloodshed. He then joined the Mount Royal Rifles, which was part of the Alberta Field Force, and served as sub-commander of Fort Edmonton.

The rebellion was short lived, lasting less than two months, and Brisebois returned to his job as a registrar. In late 1889, the land titles office was phased out and, now unemployed, Brisebois moved to Winnipeg where he died of a heart attack on February 13, 1890, just a few weeks shy of his fortieth birthday. He was buried in the Catholic cemetery in St. Boniface, Manitoba.

Brisebois is not an uncommon family name in Quebec, and there are at least four families of that name in the South Durham area today. Brisebois and Adelle Malcouronne had no children and, as far as is known, none of the Brisebois in South Durham today are related to the man who erected the fort that grew to become the city of Calgary.

P.J. Girard's Store, circa 1920. Girard's general store, located at the north
end of Main Street, opened at the turn of the twentieth century
and sold almost everything from groceries to furniture.
Notice the delivery van parked in front of the store.
(RCHS, McCarthy Collection)

CHAPTER 13

# Remembering Father Quinn

PATRICK QUINN was born on February 20, 1836. He was one of two boys in a bevy of five children born to James Quinn and Peggy Lyon. The Quinns lived in Strokestown, in the county of Roscommon, a part of Ireland that, in the early 1840s, was particularly devastated by the Great Famine.

As did so many others, the Quinns left Ireland for Canada in the hope of a better life. The family arrived at the quarantine station on Grosse Île in the summer of 1847, but only eleven year-old Patrick and his younger brother, Thomas, ever made it to the Canadian mainland. The boys' parents and three sisters died of typhus.

The orphan brothers were adopted by the Bourke family in Nicolet. Both boys went on to study at the seminary in Nicolet and both went on to be ordained into the priesthood. The brothers remained geographically close for the rest of their lives: Five years after Patrick was appointed to Richmond, Thomas became the parish priest in St. Fulgence in South Durham—less than a twenty-minute train ride from his brother's parish.

Patrick Quinn was ordained in 1862, when he was twenty-six years old. His first assignment was to St. André's parish in Acton Vale, where he served as a curate. Then, in 1864, he was made parish priest at St. Bibiane's, in Richmond, where he remained for the rest of his life. That Father Quinn became a parish priest at the age of twenty-eight should be noted. The Catholic Church in the nineteenth century had its pick of the best and the brightest; there was no higher calling than the priesthood. And, at least within the Catholic community, there was no higher authority than the parish priest.

(The role played and the prestige enjoyed by the village priest is reflected in the rectories still standing beside Catholic churches. Rarely is the house of the village priest not the grandest in the village.)

When Father Quinn moved from Acton Vale to Richmond, a forty-minute train ride in 1864, the town he arrived in looked nothing at all as it does today. For one thing, Richmond was two villages and not one town. A gazetteer published in 1873 lists Richmond East with a population of seven hundred and fifteen and Richmond Station with a population of three hundred. Each village had its own post office and, according to the gazetteer, both were "thriving."

Richmond East had grown up around Cushing Brook, a small stream (now flowing its last few hundred metres through a culvert under streets and parking lots) that spilled into the St. Francis near the Mackenzie Bridge.

Growth along the riverfront had been largely to the south of that stream, at least in part because the first bridge in the area (and the second bridge built across the St. Francis River) was erected about half a mile south of Cushing Brook.

Today, someone starting at the east abutment of the Mackenzie Bridge and travelling south on Main Street can count on one hand the buildings between the street and the river: a hot dog stand, the kayak kiosk, a two-storey brick house, and a feed mill. None of these four buildings dates back to the 1860s. Essentially, beyond the railroad tracks that run parallel to Main Street, there's only a wide wooded riparian strip to the river. It was not always so.

Through the latter half of the nineteen century and the first half of the twentieth, the strip of land between the street and the river was the site of numerous houses, shops, sheds, barns, and, in the early twentieth century, a shoe factory and a last factory. (Lasts were wooden blocks that were slipped into shoes overnight so that the shoes, made of thin leather, would maintain their shape.)

Richmond Station was of more recent vintage. A first, small Catholic mission at Brandt's Hill, part-way to Danville, gave way in 1836 to a larger, wood-clad structure carrying the same name, St. Bibiane's, but built this time on the escarpment overlooking the river. The hamlet that clustered here grew rapidly with the arrival of the station and railway yards that were installed just below the church, likely by or before 1860.

Father Quinn's parish in 1864 would have been small and struggling. The area was first settled by Americans, then made available to immigrants from Great Britain; here, as across the Townships, the first settlers were predominantly Protestant. French-speaking Catholics from the *seigneuries* along the St. Lawrence started seeping southward from 1840 on, as St-Amant pointed out. (The vast majority of *Canadiens* who moved into the Townships ended up working in the textile mills of centres like Sherbrooke and especially Magog.) Patrick Quinn's charge at first included the parishes of South Durham, Windsor, and Danville—all a short train ride away. (In 1869, his younger brother, Thomas, was assigned to the South Durham and Windsor parishes.)

In 1876, the Intercolonial Railway was completed, three decades after it was first proposed and almost a decade after it was promised to New Brunswick and Nova Scotia for joining the Confederation of Canada in 1867. This link to Halifax and the

Eastern Townships Bank, circa 1890. The light-shaded building in this view
looking north on Main Street is still a bank, although today it's the CIBC, and
it stands alone as the buildings on either side have been lost to fire or old age.
(RCHS, McCarthy Collection)

Maritimes was never a commercial success but it nevertheless
turned out to be a boon for Canada as its completion coincided
with an economic boom that was felt in Richmond and the
surrounding area. Over the course of the following few decades,
stores and houses sprang up in the area between Richmond East
and Richmond Station, creating most of the commercial section
of Richmond's Main Street that we know today.

Perhaps more important, the two villages came together in
1882 to form the Town of Richmond, even though there had
been plans to incorporate Richmond Station (or Janesville as it
is known today) as a separate municipality.

Father Quinn served his community for a full half-century, a
period that coincided with Richmond's most vigorous period of
growth and transformation. He contributed to the town's
flowering in no small way. Architecturally, no one has left more
of a stamp on Richmond than Patrick Quinn. Two of Richmond's

most imposing public buildings, and the stately house between them, were all erected under his pastoral leadership.

By the 1870s, the wood-frame church erected a scant three decades earlier was already due to be replaced. Dr. John Hayes notes that, in 1873, Bishop Laflèche of Trois-Rivières advised Father Quinn to purchase land for a cemetery and a new church.

Hayes records, "On the 22nd Oct. 1874 the executors of the estate of the late Daniel Curran, Messers James Murphy, Station Agent of the Grand Trunk Railway and William Trenholm, trader formerly of the Village of Richmond, sold another plot of a little over four acres to Rev. Patrick Quinn for the sum of two thousand dollars...part of lot no. 18 in the 14th Range of the Township of Cleveland..."

The site chosen for the wood-frame church erected in 1836 was symbolic and strategic; on an escarpment overlooking the St. Francis River, the church was situated above the valley floor where later the rail yards would be laid. The same site had earlier been identified as a location for a British fort that, had it been built, would have commanded and controlled the St. Francis just as the citadel at Quebec City dominated river traffic on the St. Lawrence.

In May 1880, six years after the adjoining four acres had been purchased, Bishop Racine of Sherbrooke wrote to Father Quinn, giving the parish priest permission to embark on the construction of a new church. The site of the old church was judged too strategic to abandon, and the new church necessitated the demolition of the old one. Services were held in an old barn after the church was demolished. It's not clear exactly when the first mass was celebrated in the new brick-clad, slate-roofed church, which today is the distinctive and picturesque landmark seen when entering Richmond on eastbound Highway 116.

The cost of the new building would have been considerable; it was after all, a big building: one hundred and twenty-seven-and-a-half feet long and fifty-seven feet wide. The bell ordered for the new St. Bibiane's weighed just over fifteen hundred pounds. It's clear that the church was completed on a pay-as-you-go basis. While in use long before then, the interior of the church was not finished until 1891, and it took another two years before the Stations of the Cross were installed. As for St. Bibiane's Casavant organ, still in regular use, and still much appreciated on special occasions, it was 1905 before the parish was able to pay for its installation.

The four acres of land that Father Quinn purchased were put to good use. Even before the church was finished, construction began on a teaching convent, Mont St. Patrice—today the town's signature building—that opened its doors in 1884. Similarly, the rectory—a still-attractive, imposing, two-storey brick house that sits between the church and former convent, though closer to Main Street than either building—was built one year after the convent.

Nor was the new St. Bibiane's the only church that bears Father Quinn's stamp. Just as, early in his pastorate, he held services in Windsor and Danville, so too, did he establish a mission in Rockland. On land donated by Williamson and Crombie—lumber barons who had made of nearby Kingsbury a thriving centre that manufactured cedar shingles and wooden butter boxes—Father Quinn established St. Malachy of Melbourne, which, like so many other churches, has since disappeared.

Besides buildings, Father Quinn gave rise to at least two institutions that continue to exist in Richmond today. In 1877, with James Murphy of the Grand Trunk Railway and several others, he founded the St. Patrick's Society. In part, the Society was created in response to the movement of Protestant Orangemen, in part a reflection of the prominence of benevolent societies at a time when these provided a social safety net. Three years later, Father Quinn, whose congregation in the 1870s was already slightly more *Canadien* than Irish, was similarly instrumental in founding the Société St-Jean-Baptiste.

There is no doubt that both the St. Patrick's Society and the Société Saint-Jean-Baptiste were also very helpful in raising the funds necessary to undertake the parish priest's building projects.

Father Quinn did not give up his charge until 1914. He served a full fifty years as parish priest, finally taking his retirement at the age of seventy-eight.

It's interesting to speculate just why Father Quinn never left Richmond. No other priest, among the two dozen who have had charge of St. Bibiane's parish, has served nearly as long. (Luke Trahan, Quinn's predecessor has the second longest tenure; he was in Richmond for a relatively modest fourteen years.)

Patrick Quinn died on March 11, 1915, less than a year after taking his retirement.

Today, a small side street, directly across from the imposing buildings he inspired, bears his name.

# CHAPTER 14

# The College and the Convent

Two of richmond's stateliest buildings stand at opposite ends of the town. Both are solid brick structures erected on escarpments overlooking the St. Francis, sites that symbolized and reflected the importance and esteem accorded to their particular vocation.

Early settlers to the Townships put down their roots progressively. The first task was to provide shelter. The second was to clear land and create fields for crops. The third, if possible, was to build a mill to grind corn or saw wood. Just as the physical needs of survival were being assured, the settlers continued the collective task of tending to the spiritual needs of their community. They started by erecting meeting houses, structures that served both as places of worship on Sundays and places of learning during the week.

Spiritual needs were never neglected. The earliest settlers held strongly to their nuanced interpretations of the Word of God. Religion was of paramount importance to them; they were direct descendants of people who had fled religious persecution in England. Sunday was observed as best as circumstances permitted: in Protestant homes the family would gather to listen to readings from the Bible; in Catholic homes it would be to kneel and recite the rosary together.

St. Francis College, circa 1882. This neatly staged photo—note the students
draped casually on many of the window sills—was likely taken in 1882 (or
shortly thereafter), when the second St. Francis College was erected.
(RCHS, McCarthy Collection)

Education was hardly less important to the earliest settlers,
even if that education meant learning to read from the only
book in the house, the family Bible. Books were considered pre-
cious and the education to be gleaned from reading was much
esteemed. A clear indication is that in 1815 the Craig Union
Library was founded. This was not a bricks and mortar building
but rather a collection of books, no more than several dozen at
the inception, which were carefully housed with one of the
Library trustees and lent out to members as requested.

Where a few families lived close by, a classroom would be
improvised in a family home. The first instruction given in
Richmond was in the house of Elmore Cushing the year following his arrival.

The first school house in the Richmond area was built in 1807
at the southern extremity of the town where we now find

St. Anne's cemetery, near the site of the first St. Anne's Anglican Church, which was erected in 1828.

Of the earliest schools in the area, only one survives. Referred to as the Old Stone Schoolhouse, the small structure that sits on the west bank of the St. Francis, at Pierce's Crossing, where the rail line crosses the river, was originally built as a meeting house. As a place of worship, it served at least four denominations.

At one time, there was a little red schoolhouse near the site of St. Bibiane's Church. Both Upper and Lower Melbourne had their own small schoolhouses. And, just as the Stone House in Denison Mills served as a schoolhouse, there is a small wood-frame house on Donnelly Street that also once served as a schoolhouse.

By the middle of the nineteenth century, there was a scattering of churches in the community: Presbyterians, Congregationalists, Methodists, Anglicans, and Catholics, among others; all had their own places of worship either on the Richmond or the Melbourne side of the river.

In addition to one and two-room schoolhouses in the area that offered a primary education, there were also academies, offering secondary education, and model schools, offering teacher training, that tried to establish themselves. If a young man chose to pursue his studies, he would be sent to one of the New England colleges or to Montreal. By the 1850s, the community was ready for higher learning, especially since fifty kilometres up-stream, the people of Lennoxville had opened the doors of Bishop's University in 1845.

In 1854, the Parliament of Great Britain granted a charter to St. Francis College and in 1855 the fledgling institution opened its doors. Appropriately enough, the land on which it was built originally formed part of the property first accorded to Elmore Cushing.

From the start, St. Francis College set out to distinguish itself as being a little different. Education in the nineteenth century

Richmond Men's Hockey Team. In 1903, when this photo was taken, hockey
teams were seven a side; the seventh player being the rover.
The team had only one substitute. Women's teams were equally common.
(RCHS Archival Collection)

was an offshoot of religion. Bishop's University was an Anglican
institution, and one of its primary aims was to train young men
for the clergy. In contrast, St. Francis College was interdenominational from the start, perhaps a reflection of the religious divers-
ity of the area. An even more radical position was taken by the
College in 1872, when it made a short-lived attempt to become
co-educational and admitted women as well as men. From 1858
to 1898, it was affiliated with McGill University and during that
time it offered agricultural courses, business degrees, and normal school programs to train teachers.

The building that opened its doors in 1855 was much smaller
than the building that sits there today. It was a more cube-like
structure stretching four stories high. It had classroom space to
accommodate one hundred students and dormitory space for

forty boarders, as well as private living quarters for the principal and his family. In 1882, the original St. Francis College burned to the ground.

A second building, with slightly different lines but approximately of the same size and shape, was erected on the same site. It served first as the college it was designed to be, and then, at the turn of the twentieth century, as St. Francis College High School. In 1942, after sixty years of wear and tear, the second building was torn down and a third, much larger, building was erected in its place. It is that third building that we see today at the top of the hill on College Street. Identified over its seldom-used front doors as St. Francis High School, it has in fact been St. Francis Elementary School since the construction of the Regional High School in 1968.

At the north end of town, at *1010 rue Principale*, stands the Town's other stately brick building, a structure that has undergone both greater and lesser changes than St. Francis College. Le Couvent Mont Saint-Patrice was built on the initiative of Father Patrick Quinn, and named in his honour. It opened in 1884 as a boarding school for girls. The original building, four storeys high, brick-clad and slate-roofed, was a quarter of the size of the building that stands there today. It was designed and built by two brothers, Alexandre and Cyrias Ouellette, who, with their crew, began construction in July of 1883 and finished fourteen months later in September of 1884. The cost of erecting the building was seventy-five hundred dollars.

The Convent was the second of three buildings that Father Quinn erected on a bluff overlooking the rail yards and the river. First, he oversaw the construction of St. Bibiane's Church in 1882, then the Convent in 1884, and finally the rectory in 1885.

It's also worth noting that the Bishop of Sherbrooke, Antoine Racine, gave Father Quinn permission to embark on the construction of the Convent only after a school for boys had been built. What came to be known as the Brothers' School, as it was run and staffed by the Brothers of the Sacred Heart, was built in 1882 on Main Street, just south of the corner of Adam Street. Today the building serves largely as an apartment block although it accommodates two storefronts as well; only the modified form of the old bell tower on the front facade hints at its scholastic origins.

Why Father Quinn chose to reserve the much more prestigious site next to the church for the Convent, rather than use it for a boys' school is not clear and is perhaps a little surprising. The Roman Catholic Church was (and remains) a systemically paternalistic institution that exclusively favoured males. Father Quinn might have been expected to situate a seminary rather than a convent next door to the church. It can be speculated that Bishop Racine's vision, and not that of Richmond's parish priest, accounts for Le Couvent Mont Saint-Patrice sitting where it does.

Hardly a decade before, in 1875, Bishop Racine had established the Séminaire Saint-Charles next door to the Cathédrale St-Michel in Sherbrooke. Both seminaries and convents served two purposes: one was to provide secondary schooling to those who could afford it; the second was to cull the graduating classes for possible candidacy for further study that would lead to holy orders. It may well be that with a seminary in Sherbrooke, Bishop Racine was disinclined to establish a second seminary a short distance away in Richmond. However, a convent at that distance could be seen as ideal: families from further away could send their sons and daughters off to boarding school on the same train, with the girls disembarking at Richmond, forty minutes or so before the boys got off in Sherbrooke.

Whatever the case, it was the Convent that was built on the bluff overlooking the river. Father Quinn invited Les Sœurs de la Congrégation de Notre-Dame de Montreal (CND) to staff and administer the girls' school. The school and land belonged to the parish until 1897, at which time the CND purchased the building. The nuns immediately enlarged the Convent, approximately by half, through the addition of a wing. Seven years later, in 1904, a second wing was added, giving the building its present configuration as seen from Main Street. These first two additions were so seamlessly affixed to the original building that even a trained eye finds it all but impossible to tell where the original building ended and the annexes were added. A final addition was made to the Convent in 1922 when a squat, industrial-looking block was erected behind the pinion-roofed main building where it could remain, functional but unsightly, aesthetically inoffensive from the street.

If the Convent has undergone fewer external changes than the College that burned once and was rebuilt twice, it has undergone far greater changes within its walls.

The Convent archives reveal that on August 21, 1884, four nuns arrived from Montreal to start classes that September. Finishing touches had yet to be put to the building, but news of its construction had aroused more interest than anticipated. When the doors opened, the nuns were overwhelmed: there were fifteen boarders and one hundred and thirty-eight day students anxious to register, with more applications arriving each passing day. On October 12, two more nuns arrived from the Mother House as reinforcements.

Despite the additions made to the building over the years, the Convent seemed often to be overcrowded with as many as forty students crammed into what were in some instances small, improvised classrooms. The school population reached its peak just before it began its slow slide into demise; during the 1950-

1951 school year, the Convent housed seventy boarders and accommodated an additional two hundred and thirty-five day students. In the fall of 1951, a new elementary school, L'École Sainte-Famille (a building we now know as the CLSC), opened its doors, as did, three years later, a co-educational high school, Notre-Dame des Écoles (now standing empty on Adam Street). Both new schools siphoned off students from the Convent.

Just as St. Francis College had started as an interdenominational institution that accepted students of all faiths, the Convent started as a bilingual school teaching both official languages. This decision was made by the nuns of the CND who were committed to serving the entire Catholic community, and at the time the Catholic population would have been quite evenly split between English and French speakers.

When the Convent first opened, the nuns' vocation was to prepare the young women in their charge to become good housewives, save those who felt an inclination to become a teaching or a nursing sister, or were seen by the nuns to have qualities and aptitudes for those fields. (Only after the end of World War II did the practice of calling all nurses 'sister', whether they were nuns or not, die out.) Girls were taught catechism, English, French, home economics, arithmetic, art, history and geography.

Art encompassed theatre, painting, and music; it was the teaching of music that seemed to take particular hold at the Couvent Mont St-Patrice. Today, it is the only discipline that continues to be taught there.

At the beginning of the twentieth century, in keeping with changes that were slowly coming, the Convent started offering secretarial courses. For a time, it was the only school in Canada that graduated fully bilingual secretaries.

In 1964, as the Quiet Revolution swept through Quebec, the Convent found itself under new administration, that of the freshly-minted Ministry of Education. The building still belonged to the CND but its vocation was taken from the hands of the nuns. The classrooms were rented to the Morilac School Board; the teaching sisters were no longer answerable to Mother Superior, but to the administrators of the Ministry of Education.

In 1981, the Morilac School Board, faced with a declining school population, no longer needed the classroom space at the Convent. Only seven nuns still lived in the building, hardly enough to warrant the maintenance and upkeep of a twenty-five thousand square foot building with heating cost that ran to twenty-four thousand dollars annually. The nuns moved into a nearby house on Gouin Street. The Convent, owned by the Congregation's Mother House in Montreal, was going to be left empty and, unless a buyer was found, would eventually face demolition.

Almost immediately, Les Amis de la Musique de Richmond, a community-based, non-profit organization led by Jeanette Charland, formed and set out to save both the building and one aspect of its pedagogical heritage, the teaching of music.

The year after the nuns closed the Convent, the building opened again to offer music courses. Les Amis de la Musique was using a fraction of the building's cavernous space, but nevertheless managed to prove itself up to the task of maintaining both the edifice and the music school. In October of 1984, Charland's non-profit group purchased what many considered a white elephant for the sum of five thousand dollars.

Under Charland's leadership, the structure slowly started filling its voluminous space. In addition to instrumental music, courses were offered in choral singing, theatre, drawing and painting. One year after taking over the building, Les Amis de la Musique started presenting concerts. The edifice was opened up to a number of community organizations; the Volunteer Bureau, Meals on Wheels, the Cadet Corps, a day-care centre, a youth centre, the Golden Age Club, all found homes there. So too did a number of artists who found the old classrooms with their high ceilings made ideal studio space. Musicians, photographers, sculptors and painters (including Madeleine Lemire who is a member of the Royal Canadian Academy of the Arts) have all found convivial working space in the former convent at one time or another.

In 2016, a new non-profit organization using the original name Couvent Mont St-Patrice, took over the administration of the building with the intention of carrying out the extensive renovations needed to bring it up to code. The group's aim is to preserve the exterior look of the landmark building but make the interior better respond to the various needs of the community organizations that it now houses. Still at home in the building is the Centre d'Art de Richmond, the same non-profit that Charland created under a different name. Music continues to animate at least a small part of the building.

# CHAPTER 15

# John Hayes and the New Bridge

I N 2009, when the newer of the two bridges spanning the St. Francis River at the junction of Highways 116, 143, and 243 was officially named Le pont Frederick-Coburn, one voice in the wilderness, a former president of the Richmond County Historical Society (RCHS), suggested that a more appropriate name would have been Le pont John-Hayes.

It's true that Frederick Simpson Coburn (1871-1960) is a name that is known internationally, albeit within that rather small subset of people who collect or know Canadian art. The name is still recognized in art galleries and mentioned in art history texts. Seven or eight decades ago, F. S. Coburn was arguably the name most readily associated with Canadian Art.

As for Dr. John Hayes (1846-1932), his name, long forgotten, was never known much beyond Richmond and the Eastern Townships. However, during his lifetime, he was very prominent in Richmond, and his contributions to the community he served were such that it would have been entirely appropriate to commemorate his name with a bridge.

Hayes seems to have been a most dynamic and remarkable man. He was born in 1846 in Quebec City to Irish parents and came to Richmond as a child. He first attended what was known

Coney Island, circa 1890. Some dozen miles upstream from Richmond, Coney Island was a very popular tourist attraction at the turn of the twentieth century when recreational use of the river was at its peak. (RCHS, McCarthy Collection)

as the Little Red Schoolhouse that once stood not far from the first St. Bibiane's Church, and then went to St. Francis to complete his high school. His medical studies seem to have brought him as far as Padua, in northern Italy, but he returned to Richmond to establish a medical practice. It was here he married Agnes Dohan with whom he raised five children. Hayes practiced medicine at a time when—at all hours of the day or night—doctors made house calls, or were visited at their homes by patients well enough to get there on their own. Beyond his professional life, he was president of both the Richmond Catholic School Commission and the Eastern Townships Historical Society. He was elected mayor of Richmond on five occasions between 1902 and 1923. Fluent in both official languages, he wrote articles for the *Sherbrooke Daily Record* and *La Tribune de Sherbrooke*.

Most interesting for us today, he was also an enthusiastic amateur historian.

In the archives of the RCHS are housed more than a dozen boxes, each laden with stacks of large, manila envelopes that contain reams upon reams of papers filled with Hayes's very neat calligraphic notes. Similarly, the Société d'histoire de Sherbrooke also has considerable archival material from John Hayes.

(The RCHS came by its material quite memorably. Two of its members—Esther Healy and Sharon Shaw—were working well into the evening on July 1, 1998. The two were painting an upstairs room at the RCHS, preparing it for a new exhibit, when, at nine o'clock at night, a surprising visitor arrived. She was a granddaughter of Hayes, and was married to Sam Elkas, who had served as Quebec's Minister of Transportation during Robert Bourassa's second stint as premier. She had donations for the museum: boxes and boxes of her grandfather's papers, as well as a very large pen and ink drawing of the University of Padua done by her grandfather.)

Surprisingly, given the extent of the Hayes collections at the RCHS and the Société d'histoire de Sherbrooke, there are yet more papers and photographs left by Hayes to be found in Richmond. In 1983, Jean-Roch Lapointe purchased a three-storey, red-brick house on Main Street, directly across from St. Bibiane's Catholic Church. The house had been built by Hayes in 1891 or earlier, and had remained in the Hayes family for nine decades. When Lapointe moved into the newly emptied house, he found a number of discarded family photos and, in a wooden kindling box in the basement, a very considerable collection of papers.

Lapointe sorted them by content into almost two dozen large manila envelopes, each neatly identified: Father Quinn's jubilee, St. Patrice Convent and St. Bibiane's Church, Craig's Road,

McKenzie Bridge, Pioneers of the Townships, the first Catholic school, early Townships newspapers, and Congregational Churches. Some of the manila envelopes hold published material: copies from the 1930s of the *Quebec Chronicle-Telegraph* and *Le Soleil de Québec*, yellowed newspaper clippings from the *Sherbrooke Daily Record* and *La Tribune de Sherbrooke* penned by Hayes; and a small, thirty-two-page booklet, written in French and co-authored by Hayes, on writers of the Eastern Townships (the doctor's contribution being short biographical sketches of seventy-seven writers divided by genre: historians, poets, science writers, novelists, and statesmen).

Some clippings provide a glimpse of how meticulous Hayes was: On July 9, 1913, the Sherbrooke Daily Record published an article by Hayes entitled Pioneers of the Townships Press. Hayes kept two copies of the article; but he also kept two copies of a letter to the editor from L.C. Bélanger who provided a different account of the first French-language newspaper in the Townships, and finished his argument with a flourish of Latin. Hayes replied to Bélanger's retort, but kept only one copy of his reply. We assume the doctor got the last word.

The overwhelming majority of the material Lapointe found consists of countless sheets of paper filled with Hayes' very legible and almost faultless handwriting. Hayes wrote in ink with a straight pen, or possibly a fountain pen, and only on one side of the sheet. Much of the paper that Hayes wrote on bore letterheads. It's easy to explain his own letterhead, John Hayes M.D. Richmond, but how did he come to have so much paper bearing the words 'Grand Trunk Railway System' or 'Queen Insurance Company of America Agency' or 'Jos. Bedard & Sons General Merchants'? Why did he invariably use the American spelling of words like 'colour' or 'honour' rather than the British spelling? And why did he often end a sentence with a long dash rather than a period?

There are some frustrations for the reader. Hayes never dated his work. The occasional newspaper clipping includes a date, but never does he indicate a date on his handwritten papers. We can't tell if he wrote about the Craig Union Library before he wrote about the Methodist Church, or if he was interested in the Mechanics' Institute before he began writing the Annals of the Catholic Church in Richmond.

Similarly, because he was writing for his contemporaries, his geographical points of reference are of little use to us today. For example, Hayes writes, "As early as 1816 the Methodists built a 'union meeting house' in Melbourne, the remains of which are yet visible in the angle of the road near Capt. Rose's farm (now occupied by Mr. J. Dionne)." To know where the Captain and Mr. Dionne lived! To know what angle in what road!

Potentially more problematic is that Hayes never numbered his pages. His texts on different topics are kept together most frequently by straight pins in the top left hand corner of the sheaf of papers. These have rusted with time and only the most sure-fingered researcher is going to attempt removing a pin to better read the clump of pages. Other pages are held together by butterfly pins and, more rarely, paper clips. Fortunately, it is only the rare sheet of paper which is found floating loosely.

Hayes wrote copiously. He was a dedicated amateur historian who acknowledged his sources and assiduously chronicled memorable events. For example, when Father Quinn celebrated fifty years in the priesthood in 1912, he was widely feted and among other tributes received a warm congratulatory letter from Bishop Paul Laroque of Sherbrooke; Hayes translated the letter into English for his own notes.

Following World War I, or the Great War as Hayes would have known it, he made what seems to be an exhaustive list of the young men from the Richmond area who served in the war, allotting each man a short biographical sketch of a page or so.

His interest in history was accompanied by an active participation in politics. Through the first few decades of the twentieth century, Richmond elected its mayors for one-year and two-year terms. The Town also adopted the practice of regularly alternating between English-speaking and French-speaking mayors. These factors explain his five short stints at the helm of the town: 1902-1903, 1910, 1914, 1920, and 1923. Hayes' multiple terms suggest he was a popular mayor, but his popularity seems not to have radiated quite as far as he might have liked. He ran for provincial office in 1923 and for a federal seat in 1911 and 1926, but his political career never went beyond the municipal level.

It's easy to imagine that one of the highlights of the doctor's political career came in 1903, during his first term of office, when a new bridge was erected across the St. Francis River, linking Richmond to Melbourne. This was the third bridge to be built between the two villages. As mentioned earlier, a wooden bridge, erected in 1847, was succeeded by a metal one in 1882. This second bridge was badly damaged in 1889 and then swept completely away in 1901. People went back to crossing by scow, a wide, flat-bottomed boat that was poled across the river—when conditions permitted.

Hayes, as mayor of Richmond, was very much at the centre of the inauguration of the new bridge (officially called the Mackenzie Bridge, but better known as the Old Bridge or the Green Bridge, it's the preferred bridge of most locals). Meticulous as he was about not throwing out any papers, it is not surprising that Hayes kept the speech he delivered when the bridge was opened.

This is what Dr. John Hayes, mayor of Richmond, told his fellow citizens and invited guests on May 25, 1903, at the Richmond Fair Grounds (the site today of the community centre, the arena and the baseball diamond) where part of the festive day's events were being held:

The presence of this large concourse of citizens here to-day to do honor to the memory of that good and dearly loved Queen, Victoria, whose name is a household word throughout the lands, as well as to celebrate in a manner befitting the importance of the event, the official opening of the New St. Francis Bridge under such favourable auspices is a subject, no doubt, of gratification to us all.

I take this occasion to extend, on behalf of the Citizens of Richmond, whom I have the honor to represent and in the names of the Bridge Board to the Honorable Gentlemen members of the Provincial Cabinet and their colleagues in the Legislature, to the Mayors and members of the different Municipal Councils, who have come to assist us in this demonstration, and to you all a most hearty welcome.

I have reason to feel proud of the honor you have conferred on us by your presence; I have reason to feel proud of this day marking as it does an epoch in the annals of this community.

The disaster of that eventful Sunday, April [date missing in original text] 1901, is too vividly impressed on your minds to necessitate my recalling it. Free Communication between the banks of the St. Francis River was once again interrupted.

A generous people was deprived of free intercourse, trade was impeded and altogether the condition of these municipalities was deplorable indeed.

The old Bridge Company had lost everything in the disaster, and notwithstanding its good will, was unable to rebuild. I believe I echo the sentiments of all present when I say that public sympathy was entirely with the company in its misfortune.

Outside capital could not be induced to undertake what appeared to be a hazardous enterprise, it soon became manifest that if ever the St. Francis Bridge was to be re-constructed, the three Municipalities interested must undertake the task either alone or with Government assistance.

This idea was actively promulgated by our Member, Mr. Mackenzie, and I deem it my duty to compliment him on the manner in which he has performed his parliamentary duties, in and out of the House, in this connection. Through his untiring energy and indefatigable zeal a large measure of the success of this enterprise is due. To Mr. McKenzie therefore and to the Provincial Government we owe our sincere thanks for the substantial grant of fifteen thousand dollars.

On behalf of the Bridge Board, I may say that we have looked forward eagerly and with anticipation of unalloyed pleasure to the day when we could say that our labors were ended; that the inconveniences, the worries and dangers of the past two years were buried in the joys of this inauguration.

Our task was a comparatively easy one, under the guidance of Mr. Wm. Ross, Inspector, and Mr. L.L. Vallée, the government engineer, whose artistic talent and engineering skill have produced this magnificent structure, a gem indeed in the emerald setting of the Melbourne Hills.

I am aware that there has been a certain amount of opposition to the scheme. I ask you gentlemen who have opposed it to

—Let the dead past bury its dead

—Act—act in the living present

—Hearts within and God o'erhead

Act, that is to say to put forth our best efforts for the welfare of this community, for that of our native province which has sent us some of her most distinguished sons to participate in our official opening, and for Canada, our common country.

—Hearts' within—that is hearts united in a common effort for the good of all. We have spanning the St. Francis River to-day tangible evidence of what can be done by united action. May I hope that this union, which has accomplished so much in the past, may be continued into the future, for the best interests of all.

—God o'erhead—I trust that providence will not look unfavorably on our work and that the new St. Francis Bridge will long remain on its rock foundations, a thing of beauty and a joy forever.

I have one more wish to express, I know it cannot be realized, nevertheless I wish that all here present will be present also when this bridge will have attained its majority and will be declared free.

Funeral Cortege, circa 1890. This house, belonging to the Cross Undertakers
on Stanley Street, is architecturally identical today although
it has long since given up its vocation as a funeral parlour.
(RCHS Archival Collection)

The mayor's speech, it is easy to imagine, was very warmly
applauded by the Members of the Legislative Assembly, the
Mayors and Councillors, and all those present.

Hayes was present—but not as the Town's mayor—in 1913
when the bridge "attained its majority" and was "declared free,"
that is, was fully paid for and users were no longer required to
pay a toll to cross it.

Hayes was eighty-six when he died in Richmond on August
19, 1932. His five children—four boys and a girl—all remained
in the area. Redmond Hayes, who practiced law in Montreal
before returning to Sherbrooke to become a judge, came to own
the family house in Richmond though it was his brother,
Harold, who lived there. It was the estate of Redmond Hayes
that sold the house to Jean-Roch Lapointe.

As for John Hayes, while there is no bridge named after him,
a small street in Richmond's industrial park carries his name.

Main Street from the St. Jacob's Hotel, circa 1910. The building on the right
was the St. Jacob's Hotel. It was transformed into a rooming
house in the 1990s and was lost to fire in 2017.
(RCHS, McCarthy Collection)

# CHAPTER 16

# John Hayes, Part 2
## *Plus ça change*

WE HAVE ALREADY SEEN that, as well as a medical doctor, John Hayes was also an amateur historian, a chronicler of his times, and a careful archivist who seems to have kept almost every piece of paper that passed though his hands.

A century later, the Hayes Collection in the Archives of the Richmond County Historical Society offers some surprising parallels to contemporary political practices. The doctor's meticulousness permits a look back at the federal election of 1911 in which he ran as a candidate for the Liberal-Conservatives, one of more than half a dozen fringe parties that presented candidates that year.

The issue of the day in 1911 was reciprocity: should Canada enter into a "free trade" deal with the United States, or should the country's closest ties continue to be with the United Kingdom and the British Commonwealth? Unlike the situation in 1988, when the Conservative government of Brian Mulroney led the country into a Free Trade deal with the Americans, in 1911 the roles were reversed. The Liberal Party favoured close economic ties with the country's southern neighbour while the Conservative Party was very leery of American hegemony and wanted to remain staunchly loyal to England.

In 1911, the Liberals, under Wilfrid Laurier, had been in power for fifteen years. They enjoyed a majority of seats in Parliament when Laurier called the 1911 election, earlier than necessary. The Conservatives, under Robert Borden, had created enough of a fuss in Parliament that Laurier was prompted to give the entire country a say in the matter of reciprocity. The election was, to a large extent, a referendum of sorts on this one question.

It's not clear what prompted Hayes to become a candidate for the Liberal-Conservatives, or exactly what platform this small party was promoting. The Liberal-Conservatives had elected three members to Parliament in 1908, a number that would be reduced to one in 1911.

In Richmond-Wolfe, Hayes was running against Edmund William Tobin, a Liberal who had first been elected in 1900 and who would go on to represent the riding until 1930.

One interesting glimpse into this election held more than a century ago is a schedule for a series of debates between John Hayes and Edmund Tobin. Between August 24 and September 14 of 1911, the two men met sixteen times in towns and villages across the riding: Danville, Disraeli, Kingsbury, Wotton, and a dozen others. No doubt the absence of radio, television and social media rendered public meetings both desirable and necessary. For voters, the opportunity to see two candidates together on the same stage would have likely made the choice far easier than it is for us today, when we are unlikely to see more of a candidate than a poster stapled to a telephone pole.

Among the papers left by Hayes, two are particularly revealing.

The first is an unsigned note from the Liberal-Conservative Club of Montreal, dated September 15, 1911: "Be especially careful," it reads, "that the men you select as your representatives in the polling stations are only such as can be implicitly relied upon; in many cases they should not be chosen until the night before the election." The note goes on to reassure that the campaign is going well, but warns that danger is posed by "...the spending of enormous sums of money by our opponents during the last week of campaign."

The other is a letter signed by someone, likely Hayes' campaign manager, whose signature is illegible: "You are to take dinner with Leonard Gale tomorrow; he will put up your horses for you. In talking to Gale make the remark that his store would seem to be the proper place for the Post Office, that must be said when no one is round."

Hayes kept this letter as he kept the poll-by-poll results from election night, and the several very sympathetic letters from friends and supporters following his loss to Tobin.

If History doesn't always provide answers, it certainly raises questions. Did Hayes dine with Gale? Or was he waylaid by a medical emergency that kept him in Richmond? Did he casually—in private—make the observation that Gale's store would be a good place for the post office? Or did he ignore his political masters? Did he remain a perfect Victorian gentleman and refuse to resort to false promises?

Whatever the case, Hayes lost and Laurier lost. Canada remained staunchly British for a while longer.

The election results were dramatic and unbalanced. Borden's Conservatives won sixty percent of the seats in Parliament, a strong majority. Was the population so strongly opposed to reciprocity with the United States? The popular vote was far closer: Conservatives garnered forty-nine percent to the Liberals' forty-six percent. (The other five percent of the popular vote went to the several fringe parties; between them, they won five seats.)

This electoral loss seems not to have taken the wind out of the doctor's sails. He ended up losing two more elections, one provincial and one federal. Locally, he remained popular and was elected to his last term as mayor in 1923, when he was seventy-seven years old. He died in Richmond on August 19, 1932 at the age of eighty-six.

CHAPTER 17

# The Melbourne Township Murder

S UDDEN, violent death at the hands of another human occurs but infrequently in this corner of the world. Avery Denison was the first settler in the area to be murdered, although the murder itself occurred near Trois-Rivières.

Another exception to prove the rule occurred on a railway track that was being constructed between Kingsbury and Windsor at the turn of the twentieth century. It was a murder that faintly echoed that of Denison in that the victim was from outside the area: Denison was passing through Trois-Rivières on his way home; Ralph Andosca, the twelve-year old murdered on August 16, 1905, was here temporarily, part of a New England railway construction crew made up primarily of Italian immigrants.

The headline in *The Sherbrooke Daily Record* on Thursday, August 17, 1905, was comprehensive: "Boy Shot Down in Cold Blood / Another boy murder this time at the construction camp of the OMR [Orford Mountain Railroad] a few miles from Windsor Mills / Shot from horse by unknown Italian / May have been in Revenge for grievance against father / Murderer has escaped / High Constable Moe and Coroner Bachan Investigating."

The shooting of Ralph Andosca was all the more shocking for readers of *The Record* because of two other prominently reported criminal acts: an attempted robbery a month before on the same OMR line, and the murder, just three days before, of another adolescent in Farnham, less than seventy kilometres south-west of Melbourne.

On July 18, 1905, *The Record* headline read "Shooting on Orford Mountain Railway / Desperados attack paymaster at Construction Camp near Windsor Mills / Seriously wound him and shoot his horse dead."

Workers at the time received their wages in cash, on a monthly basis. The paymaster for the OMR was a Mr. Percy. He set out on horseback, with his son, carrying seventeen thousand dollars in bills and coins. The OMR track was being laid by several crews working simultaneously on different sections of the fifteen kilometres of track.

As Percy and his son were approaching a work camp, two armed men stepped out of the woods and demanded the payroll. Percy and his son grabbed their cash-filled satchels, abandoned their horses and ran. The attackers, identified as Italians, fired at Percy but killed the horse he was on and not him. (The horse, *The Record* points out, belonged to Dr. McCabe of Windsor.) Percy was wounded but not seriously (contrary to *The Record* headline). The two attackers, seeing their plan foiled, turned and ran. The gun shot and cries had alerted a construction crew and those men had come running. No money was stolen but that didn't diminish the seriousness of the incident. For the people in neighbouring Melbourne and Richmond, it was a little too close to home.

The second incident, the first child murder, was reported on Monday, August 14, 1905. The font-page headline of *The Record* read: "Foul Murder at Farnham, Quebec / 14 year-old boy found in lumber yard near station with brains battered out by stone."

The boy was Wilfrid Audett. He was the son of Farnham's secretary treasurer and he was working for the summer as a night call boy for the Canadian Pacific Railway. The newspaper reported him as being big for his age and known to be strong. As a call boy, his job was to run to the homes of engineers and firemen to call them to work when train crews were needed. He had left the station to call such a crew shortly after midnight on Saturday and never returned. His body was found on Sunday morning. There were signs of a struggle that indicated the young man had been set upon by two or even three assailants.

The murder was as mysterious as it was violent. There was no evident motive for the crime and no reason to explain why a fourteen-year-old should be a target.

A week later, three hobos were arrested in Hull on suspicion that they might have been responsible for Wilfrid Audett's murder, but they were soon released. The murder remained unsolved.

The killing of Ralph Andosca was equally mysterious.

Incorrectly identified as Drake in the August 17 edition of *The Record*, Ralph was the second youngest of several sons of Frank Andosca, who, as *The Record* explained, "ran the canteen." Ralph, at age twelve, is described as "an errand boy around the camp," and was likely on the verge of being expected to do a man's work.

He was killed late in the afternoon, riding a horse back to its owner, James Todd, a nearby farmer. He was a few dozen yards behind a horse and cart being driven by Todd's son, when he was shot in the back.

The Todd boy turned and saw someone, supposedly an Italian, disappearing into the woods. The shot attracted men from the nearby camp, but they were unarmed, and reluctant to attempt to catch an armed murderer.

*The Record* article questions whether the murder of an innocent twelve year-old might have been an act of revenge against the boy's father. If running the canteen meant that Frank Andosca was the camp cook, then he would have been in a position to make both friends and enemies. Lumber and construction crews might be comprised of one hundred or more labourers and their continued strength and good health depended on the camp cook. Lumberjacks were known to sign on with particular camps because of the cook. In his own way, Andosca, the camp cook, might have been as important as the camp foreman.

What is particular about *The Record* story is its xenophobia with respect to the railway's foreign workers. It's noteworthy that Andosca and the work crew are identified as Italians, yet they were all from the New England states. While immigrants, it's safe to assume that many of them had been in the United States for some time. That Andosca would have a son named Ralph (or Drake) indicates that he had been in America long enough to have become anglicized. Frank is the English equivalent of Franco, but there are no obvious Italian equivalents of Ralph and Drake, both unabashedly Anglo-Saxon names.

*The Record* article reads:

> The ways of the Italian desperado are peculiar and it is not improbable that the boy was shot as a means of striking the father.
>
> These foreigners engaged in railway construction are a desperate lot. There are about a hundred on the OMR. Scarcely a day passes without a fight among themselves. These fights are not of the Canadian variety. Their temperament has not changed under the cooler atmosphere of Canada. An injury imagined or real, instantly fires them with a desire for revenge. Their anger does not subside with the going down of the sun. It is nursed day by day. The opportunity to get even is patiently and sullenly awaited. A week or month or more may pass. But sooner or later, the victim will receive a blow, probably in the back, likely at night. He may not see his assailant but can safely figure that someone is paying off old scores.

And so it is believed that yesterday's murder was committed by someone who had perhaps waited long and failed to secure an opportunity to strike the father.

The same article in *The Record* offers a follow-up to the attempted robbery of a month earlier.

The paymaster went through the OMR camp yesterday and paid the men. He took no chances. He was accompanied by eight men in four teams. All to use a common expression were armed to the teeth. They carried Winchesters and revolvers. These firearms were in sight and must have been quite impressive.

The next day, July 19, *The Record* postulated another motive for Ralph's murder. The camp had been hit by a string of thefts, and it was speculated that perhaps Ralph had seen who it was who had been pilfering personal items. The boy was murdered, the paper speculated, to prevent him from identifying the thief.

About a week after the murder of Ralph Andosca, two men were arrested. Omer Ayette and George St-Pierre were relatively new to the area and were living in a makeshift shack in the woods. They had a shotgun that they claimed was used to hunt game, their principal food source. They claimed to be cutting firewood to sell, but the amount of cordwood found near their premises was so small as to make their assertion questionable. Furthermore, police found a red kerchief such as that worn by the men who'd attempted to rob Percy in July. The motive for the killing of Ralph, it was suggested, was robbery; the intended victim was really Todd's son who would have had some eighty dollars in his pockets, a month's wages for himself, his father, and the rental of their horses.

On September 15, some three weeks after being arrested, Ayette and St-Pierre were released. The gun found at the men's cabin was not the same gun used to kill Ralph. Other evidence, including an identification of the men by Todd, was judged to be too circumstantial to bring them to trial.

Ralph's body was brought back home to the United States for burial. The OMR line through Golden Bay and to Windsor Mills was completed, although it was torn up for scrap metal less than four decades later.

The Melbourne Township murder remains a mystery.

# PART 4

# THE TWENTIETH CENTURY

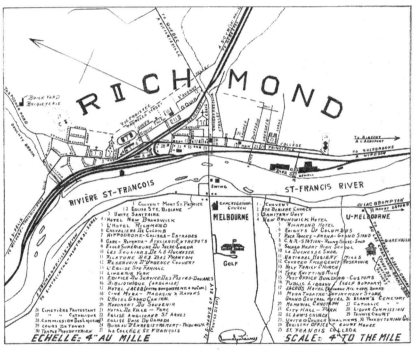

Hand Made Map of Richmond: Likely drawn during the 1930s, when La Diva Shoe had a factory on the east bank of the St. Francis, this hand-made map makes clear the importance of the railway at the time.

# CHAPTER 18

# The Native Son

FREDERICK SIMPSON COBURN is the Richmond area's most renowned native son. The designation "Richmond area" is used advisedly because the town of Richmond was not yet incorporated when Coburn was born, and Upper Melbourne was a quite distinct place. Coburn was Upper Melbourne, born and bred. His maternal grandfather was the notary, Daniel Thomas; his paternal grandfather, William Coburn, a Melbourne blacksmith. Fred Coburn left Upper Melbourne at the age of sixteen and to a very large extent lived abroad or in Montreal until the last decade of his life, yet he always kept a home in Upper Melbourne. He was internationally known, yet led a quiet, almost reclusive life, especially when he was back home in his native village. He made his name and half his fortune by painting horses, yet never owned one in his life.

Coburn was born in 1871, in the family home that stood less than fifty yards south of the Upper Melbourne Town Hall; he died in 1960, in a far more comfortable home not fifty yards north of the Town Hall. The house in which Coburn was born stood on the corner of what is now Route 243 and Cemetery Road. It was a modest, two-storey, brick structure and, like the store and post office that stood next to it, the house is long gone

Tennis Party, circa 1890. Likely taken in the late 1890s, this afternoon party
featuring games of tennis was hosted by the Mappin family.
(RCHS Archival Collection)

except for some crumbling foundations hidden by vegetation.
However, the house in which Coburn died is still standing, and
remains one of the more aesthetically notable homes in the area.

As a schoolboy, Fred would have attended a small, one-room
schoolhouse a short walk from home and later St. Francis
College across the river in Richmond. His artistic bent was
noticed early; at age ten he sold a sketch of a horse to the local
bank manager, whose horse it was, and who was so impressed
by the sketch that he offered young Fred ten dollars for it on
the spot. Later, still in his teens, he won a regional award for
penmanship. His budding talent wasn't actively encouraged
during his childhood through formal lessons, but neither was
it discouraged, so that when Coburn graduated from St. Francis
High School he went to Montreal and immediately found work
as a commercial artist.

Coburn was a natural talent, but by inclination he was also something of a scholar. In Montreal, with access to education, he promptly enrolled in evening classes at the Montreal Council of Arts and Manufacturers School where he studied commercial art. Two years later, at eighteen, he enrolled at the Carl Hecker School of Art in New York City, and two years after that he began studying fine art in Berlin, Germany. For the next several years Coburn spent time in different European cities, always studying; in London at the Slade School of Art, in Paris at the Beaux Arts. At times, as in Venice, these sojourns were very brief; at others, as in Antwerp (where he won a three-year scholarship), they were extended.

Parallel to his life as a student of fine art, Coburn was advancing a very successful career as a commercial artist. While still a teenager, he was hired for relatively noticeable projects. For example, a clipping (undated but from 1888 or 1889) from *The Sherbrooke Daily Record* announced that Coburn was doing sketches of the Patton Woollen Mills in Sherbrooke as part of a series of illustrations for Industries in Canada. The short passage finishes: "He is in the minority as regards age but ahead of the majority in his profession, and gives promise of being the most skilful artist and designer in Canada, if not on this continent."

The words turned out to be prophetic. As an illustrator, Coburn's big break came in 1896 when a chance meeting with William Henry Drummond, a medical doctor and the author of a series of very successful poems (*The Habitant* being the best-known), led to a lucrative contract with Putnam's, a major American publishing house. This was a time before screens—the silent screens of early film, the household TV screens that followed, and the ubiquitous screens of the over-connected twenty-first century—when a hard-covered, finely-bound, illustrated book was the entertainment of choice for a very wide segment of a population that was more literate than ours is today. Through Putnam's editions of works by Edgar Allan Poe, Washington Irving, Charles Dickens, and other popular authors, millions of people in the English-speaking world poured over illustrations produced by Coburn, even if they didn't necessarily know the name of the artist.

His illustrations were much in demand and provided him both with an enviable income and a reason to return home to Upper Melbourne every summer. If home was a quiet, unknown, out-of-the-way place, it was also very convenient: a short day's train trip to New York City allowed Coburn to touch base with his publishers. Until the eve of the outbreak of World War I, Coburn skipped back and forth over the Atlantic twice a year, spending his summers at home and the rest of the year in Europe. Similarly, wherever he was in Europe, he was dividing his time between illustrating and advancing his studies in painting.

The First World War marked a tremendous social change in Europe and North America; it also marked a great change in Coburn's life. Coburn found himself in Canada when war broke out; he had come home to be with his dying father, and after Newlands Coburn died in early 1915, it was neither easy nor advisable to return to Europe. However, Malvina Scheepers, whom he'd met in Antwerp almost two decades earlier and with whom he'd been in love since, came to Canada to join him. As significantly, Coburn turned his back on illustrating and focused all his energy and attention on painting.

Just as he experienced critical and financial success from the beginning as an illustrator, so too was he successful from the beginning as a painter, or almost from the beginning. After years in northern Europe, Coburn, naturally enough, painted with colours and with a style that was reminiscent of Dutch and Flemish landscape painters. In a country that, artistically speak-

Taking a break, circa 1950. Coburn (on the right) is sitting on the front steps
of his Melbourne home with George Lovett who was his friend, neighbour,
and handyman. The photo likely dates to shortly after World War II.
(Courtesy of Bob Laberge)

ing, was almost entirely Eurocentric, it was a style that was
popular with the art-buying public.

Yet, not nearly as popular as what was to come. Very early in
the 1920s, Coburn made two significant decisions. One was that
he changed his palette. Instead of the muted ochres and siennas
he had been using that typified the Dutch landscapes, Coburn
gave himself over to brighter colours: cerulean blue, viridian
green, red! The other decision was to choose the winter landscape as his theme.

The result was that Coburn went from being a Canadian artist to *the* Canadian artist. For a quarter century or more, his name was synonymous with Canadian art. The archetypical Canadian painting through the 1930s and 1940s was of a small, red, one-horse sleigh cresting over a snow-covered hill under a brilliant blue sky. Those who could afford to buy a Coburn did; those who couldn't, bought prints, cards, or calendars with reproductions of his paintings. Coburn's success was remarkable by all yardsticks. His paintings were exhibited and sold internationally. During his lifetime, he never had a solo show because his paintings sold almost as quickly as he could produce them, sometimes leaving the gallery even before the paint was fully dry. Alongside the financial success came critical success. He was made a member of the Royal Canadian Academy of the Arts and, more locally in Montreal, a member of the Pen and Pencil Club. Bishop's University awarded him an honorary degree. Perhaps the highest compliment of all for Coburn was a backhanded one: Coburn's work was so popular that forgeries of his work popped up on both sides of the Atlantic.

Coburn achieved both fame and fortune. Yet, in Upper Melbourne, where he was an annual (if seasonal) resident, Coburn was hardly known at all. Following his father's death, he bought a three-season cabin from an uncle. It had been built relatively near the river, in a flood zone, and every fall it was propped up on stilts to avoid the worst of the spring flooding. Later, in the early 1940s, he purchased a large, comfortable home across the road, that had previously been known as the Sloan Mansion. (It's now commonly known as the Coburn house and, until recently, was the home of the artist's grandniece.)

Until he gave up his Montreal apartment when he was over eighty, Coburn was in Upper Melbourne largely as a visitor. He and Malvina lived primarily in Montreal, when they were not in Europe. Following Malvina's death in 1933, Coburn never returned to Europe, but continued to spend most of his time in Montreal.

In Upper Melbourne, Coburn had only a few cousins by way of family; his own siblings (two brothers and a sister) were scattered from Ottawa to California; he had had no children with Malvina. In the years following Malvina's death, he grew very close to the Lovett family, but otherwise, for most villagers, he was something of a recluse, having all his life been a quiet and reserved personality.

By way of contrast, in Montreal he did attend at least some social events and functions. On his doctor's advice, he even took up ballroom dancing. He went on to financially support a dance studio owned by a couple professionally known as Carlotta and Alvarez. Carlotta served Coburn as a model for several years and remained a life-long friend. It was she who was with Coburn when he passed away in his home, in Melbourne, in 1960.

CHAPTER 19

# The Desmarais Family

THE LIBERAL CANDIDATE in the riding of Richmond-Arthabaska in the 2015 federal election was a fifty-year old Ottawa lobbyist, Marc Desmarais, who has deep roots in Richmond, where he was born and raised. He also has a notable political pedigree.

Desmarais' great-grandfather was Stanislas-Edmond Desmarais (1872–1948), who had a long and curiously varied political career in the first half of the twentieth century.

The Desmarais family tree stretches back to the seventeenth century and New France. By the last half of the nineteenth century, one branch of the family was farming near South Durham. Stanislas-Edmond Desmarais was one of four boys born to Médard Desmarais and his wife, Caroline Beaudoin. His first school would have been the proverbial one-room schoolhouse, or *école de rang*.

It's likely he was a good student because, at a time when many farm boys stopped attending school after the fifth or sixth grade to work on the family farm, he went on to high school in Richmond, at Les Frères du Sacré-Cœur, also known as the Brothers' School. Located on Main Street, almost at the corner of Adam, the school was the Catholic equivalent of St. Francis

Vintage Car, circa 1910. Horace Pettes Wales, sitting in the front passenger seat, was a successful merchant and the first man in Richmond to own an automobile. He retired to the family farm and when he died, in 1918, the property was bequeathed to found the retirement home that bears his name. (RCHS Archival Collection)

High School. It took about twenty minutes to get to Richmond from South Durham by train, but it's likely that Stanislas-Edmond would have boarded during the week and gone home on weekends.

He didn't return to the family farm after graduating, but found a job in Richmond, working for Horace Pettes Wales. (H.P. Wales was a successful businessman and one of Richmond's more prominent citizens, noted, among other things, for being the first person in Richmond to own a car. He was a great-grand-son of Elmore Cushing. He died childless and his estate formed the foundation of the Wales Home.)

In 1897, at the age of twenty-five, Stanislas-Edmond Desmarais went into business for himself, selling wood and coal to heat houses in the winter, then selling ice for ice-boxes in the summer.

This was still the era of the horse and wagon, or horse and sleigh, and given the nature of the merchandise he sold, Desmarais was very much in the transportation business, a business that would stay in the family for the next two generations.

While he maintained an interest in these businesses until his death, by the time he was fifty, he was no longer involved with their day-to-day operations, having turned his attention to politics.

On October 22, 1923, less than two weeks after his fifty-first birthday, Desmarais won a by-election and became the Member of the National Assembly (MNA) for Richmond. In all, he sat as Richmond's MNA for a total of seventeen years, serving from 1923 to 1935, and then again from 1939 to 1944. He waged six electoral campaigns for the provincial Liberal party, winning four of them. During his first stint in office, a period covering twelve years, he worked under Louis-Alexandre Taschereau, and during his second, under Adélard Godbout.

Desmarais was a backbencher, an MNA who served his party without rising to a ministerial post. However, what makes his political career very unusual to twenty-first century eyes is that he was simultaneously active both at the provincial and municipal levels.

From 1927 to 1929, and again from 1931 to 1933, Desmarais was mayor of Richmond even while he was a sitting MNA in Quebec City.

At the time, Richmond's mayors served two-year terms and the practice was to alternate between French-speaking and English-speaking mayors. Until the 1970s, Richmond's council minutes had entries in both official languages.

Trains ran frequently in those days and the trip by rail from Richmond to Quebec City took only a few hours. It's relatively easy to read, or even write, when you're sitting in a rail car moving at eighty or ninety kilometres per hour. For Desmarais, travel time was almost certainly synonymous with time spent at his office desk. Nevertheless, juggling two political careers must have required some creative (if not frenetic) multi-tasking, at least on occasion.

(Desmarais was not the only politician to sit simultaneously on two elected bodies. Perhaps the most notable example was Henri-Gustave Joly de Lotbinière (1829–1908) who was briefly both a member of the National Assembly in Quebec City and a Member of Parliament in Ottawa. The practice of sitting at both the provincial and federal level was abolished in 1874.)

As well as being active in the governance of his town and his province, Desmarais was involved in promoting commerce. He was involved with the local Chamber of Commerce, and also became president of the Quebec Retailers Association and the Canadian Retailers Association.

It's been almost seven decades since Desmarais passed away, yet there are people who remember him. Jérôme Desmarais was fourteen when his grandfather died, an event he remembers very clearly.

"I was at boarding school in Arthabaska," he says. "It was March, it was still cold, I was outside, playing hockey, and I was my team's goaltender. I was called off the ice and told that my grandfather was dying and that I had to get home as soon as possible. I remember getting changed and being brought to a small restaurant that doubled as the bus stop. I sat there, too shy to move, until 2:00 when the bus finally came.

"My grandfather was a good person," Jérôme continues. "He had a soft heart, he was generous, he loved kids. My first summer jobs I owed directly, or indirectly, to my grandfather. I remember delivering ice with a wagon drawn by a horse that knew all the stops along the route. I also remember delivering coal and getting home at the end of the day so covered in dust that I was literally as black as coal."

Stanislas-Edmond was also not without his quirks. "My grandfather owned the brickyard," Jérôme recalls. "He would drive a couple of us out there to turn bricks. These were laid out on shelves to dry. To cure evenly, they had to be turned ninety degrees, and then turned again and again to allow all four sides to dry. We earned a penny a shelf turning bricks. There were lots of bricks on a shelf, and our hands were pretty raw at the end of the day. But it was the ride out to the brickyard that really stays with me because my grandfather, for some reason, always tended to drive on the left hand side of the road. I remember the car swinging onto Spooner Pond Road, which was a gravel road at the time, and the car always drifting over to the wrong side of the road."

Just as his business ventures were family businesses, with his sons and grandsons continuing the companies, so too were his political campaigns family affairs with his wife and four sons all out on the campaign trail in one way or another.

"My grandmother, Joséphine Janelle, originally from Warwick," says Jérôme, "was also quite a remarkable person. She was very resourceful, very self-sufficient. At a time when few women did, she worked, at least some of the time, outside of the home. She sometimes worked in the United States for the Singer Sewing Machine Company. I also remember her going to Chicago for a conference. She was a rare breed at the time. She lived to the age of ninety-four."

Stanislas-Edmond and Joséphine were married in 1899 and together they had four children: Ola, Antonio, Gérard and Gaston.

Stanislas-Edmond Desmarais died on March 2, 1948, at the age of seventy-five.

CHAPTER 20

# Alec Crabtree Booth

A T THE FOUNDING MEETING of the Richmond County
Historical Society, on May 24, 1962, with seventy-seven
charter members present, Alec Crabtree Booth was elected one
of the group's three vice-presidents. A few years later, Alice
Dresser, the Society's founding president, passed away and
Booth came to the helm of the fledgling society.

In 1965 Booth, in his role as president, penned a sixteen-page
essay entitled *County Historical Society* and had it printed in
booklet form. The following year, under his presidency, Volume
I of *Tread of the Pioneer, Annals of Richmond County and Vicinity*
was published.

The publication of *The Annals* (Volume 1 in 1966, Volume 2 in
1968) represented not just a first flowering of the newly sprouted
Society but also the culmination of a project initiated by the
Richmond County Women's Institute. As the first paragraph of
*The Annals* notes: "At a meeting of the Richmond County
Women's Institute on October 21, 1961, a committee composed
of Miss Alice Dresser, Mrs. A. T. Smith and Mrs. S. Husk was
appointed to gather and compile a history of the county."

*The Annals*, as Booth indicates in the Dedication and
Introduction of the first volume, are "a collection of articles"

written by "many of Miss Dresser's old friends." Curiously, Booth did not contribute to *The Annals* even though he clearly worked at raising funds to cover publication costs.

Yet, it's clear from the two short works that Booth published, *County Historical Society* and *Out of My Days as a Working Man*, that he could write with sparkling wit and keen insight. In his writing, Booth comes across as being perceptive, thoughtful and insightful, but also as very witty and funny. Even when dealing with a serious topic, he will use a turn of phrase that brings a smile to the reader. The photo on the back of his book of poetry shows a man whose thin, white moustache contrasts with his dark eyes that seem to brim with youthful mischief.

The cover of his sixteen-page essay, *County Historical Society*, bears witness to the fact that fundraising has ever been with the Society. On the front cover is printed: "The profit from the sale of this essay is to be used to finance the publication of a volume of Richmond County History at present being prepared."

Opening the cover, one can read: "The cost of publication of this essay has been borne by the following friends of the Society." The ensuing list takes up an entire page and enumerates over fifty names and institutions, divided according to the towns of their provenance: Asbestos, Danville, Richmond, and Windsor. Curiously, virtually all the donors from Windsor were French while all but two of the Richmond donors were English.

A few pages into his essay, Booth, with humour, describes the demographic of his era: "The population is now for the most part French-speaking, but with isolated and diminishing English-speaking communities still existing as, let us say, ethnic and linguistic pockets of resistance. But it is an amiable resistance." Booth's description is as apt today as it was in 1965.

Closer to the end of his essay he proposes, "A historical society properly incorporated is a public body and here in the Province of Quebec ought to be bilingual." Almost half a century later, the

RCHS is still striving—with very little noticeable effect—to become truly bilingual.

This point notwithstanding, if Booth intended his essay to serve as a set of guidelines for the future functioning of the RCHS, he achieved considerable success. He mentions "a sense of history" and enumerates the several ways in which this "natural gift" reveals itself. He stresses the importance of the roles played by the archivist, the chronicler and the custodian. He describes how historical societies come by their artefacts as well as how "a historical society will miss getting something it would appreciate having" because the item has gone "to a bigger institution such as a university library." He wryly concludes the passage: "There is nothing you can do about that but gnash your teeth, somewhat difficult to do while smiling at the person who is telling you why he is not going to give this something to the society that it expected to get."

Booth's own "sense of history" expresses itself in his admiration for the early settlers, "I always have a feeling of personal inadequacy, of an inferiority to these people," but without nostalgia, warning that, "people speak frequently about the old days, seldom the good old days." Yet he is not without concerns about the future. He points out that, "the best things of the old days have been lost along with the bad," and as the population left the farms to live in towns and cities, "we have evolved from a free society to a planned society, and if life, liberty and the pursuit of happiness really comprise our aim, we may have evolved without sufficient precaution against a loss of direction."

Two decades after penning his essay, Booth published his poems. Curiously enough, the final words of his 1965 essay "... to catch sight and scent of an empty virgin land that the avarice of man had not corrupted," are picked up in the first paragraph of the Author's Foreword of *Out of My Days as a Working Man*: "We say our hope is heaven, but what we are really looking for is a Garden of Eden at the beginning of time when there were no complications. A place that the avarice of man has not corrupted, where we can be our own free selves."

*Out of My Days as a Working Man* is a slim, eighty-six-page volume. It was self-published and not dated. More than a collection of poems, Booth informs us that it is "a chap book in which the reader is not released from his responsibility of working for an understanding by reading between the lines, being in part a shout at the state of affairs or a play of poems in several indignations with sundry other unrelated ballads and somewhat sentimental sermons composed in content and discontent by Alec C. Booth. It is recommended that the poems be performed rather than perused."

The words are arranged vertically and symmetrically and several of the lines are written in full capital letters across the page. In case Booth's verbal dexterity and subtle humour don't capture our attention, the layout of the page certainly does. The poems that follow carry through on Booth's promises: he is indignant and angry, but he is also playful with his language; the poems are eclectic and provoke sudden turns of mood. Above all, the poems spark our imagination and prompt us to rethink and re-examine ourselves and our surroundings.

Booth's dedication page reads: To My Wife /Who Has Put Up With It. I/Do Not/By Modish Chatter/Change/A Simple/ Into/A Complicated Matter. To follow Booth's instructions and perform this poem, we would want two characters on the stage: Booth's exasperated wife, telling him, "*Tu compliques toujours les choses, Alec!*" and Booth, calmly and eloquently enunciating his lines. It's easy to imagine, given Booth's penchant for posing probing questions of the soul, that this scene might have played itself out innumerable times.

Booth's preoccupation with avarice, and its close cousins— greed, ambition, envy—appear suddenly and unexpectedly in several poems, including Glad Hand Samson which ends with the lines:

I'll tell you—"Glad to know you,"
—"And here's my hand my friend,"
But do not stand between me,
And my promised land,
Or you'll feel the subtle pressure,
Of my unfriendly underhand.

Much of Booth's anger and indignation is directed towards the bosses for whom he works; men who are, in Booth's eyes, both stupid (despite their academic qualifications) and corrupt. He finishes the poem, Was That Your Mind I Heard Closing, with the lines, "Oh! It's nice to be well educated,/And have nothing whatever to learn." In Hear Now! The Boss Beaver, he writes, "For why make the social pot boil,/ With opinion pro and con,/ On some silly little issue—/Concerned with right and wrong?" For Booth, the workplace itself is a "prison of production lines" where "Fifty years attention/Accumulates a pension."

Many of us may feel some degree of workplace frustration, but could we express it with as such wit and humour?

It's probably safe to assume that the poems in this collection were written over four or even five decades. Old Soldier Re-Enlisted describes the death of a superannuated soldier. The poem is all Kiplingesque, slapdash glory; a vigorous, devil-may-care ballad in which the dying soldier reflects that life's been an unexpected bounty because "...the fact is plain and clear,/It's the [bullet] I missed in Africa, in/eighteen ninety-nine." It's easy to imagine that this poem, even though placed at the end of the book, could have been written in the late 1940s or the 1950s. On the other hand, in The Predicament, the poem's narrator is not an angry underling railing against his superiors but rather "Middle aged, and middle classed,/Having made the grade at last."

In the same poem, he writes, "Why this lack of satisfaction?/ Why this yearning for distraction?" These lines remind us of the lack of direction that Booth noted in his essay.

A short essay and a book of poems, regardless of their merit, are hardly enough to keep body and soul together, let alone raise a family. Who was Alec Crabtree Booth, where did he live and what did he do?

"You have to understand that my father was born in England and even though he'd been in Canada since he was a teenager, he was very much a British Imperialist," says Ronald (Ron) Booth, Alec's son and a retired teacher who now lives in Sherbrooke. "That explains why, when WW II broke out, even though he had been studying Theology at McGill, he left university to enlist. That was where his duty lay, and he was ruled by duty, just like the waves were ruled by Britannia. He was British at heart."

Nonetheless, by 1939, part of that British heart had taken root in the Eastern Townships and, before shipping off to war in 1940, he married Rita Codère. He made it no closer to the front than London where he was stationed with a corps of mechanical engineers.

"Among his papers," Ron recalls, "were preliminary drawings for amphibious tanks capable of functioning while fully submerged."

It was during the war years that Booth acquired a range of engineering skills, and it was these that led to a twenty-five-year career at the Windsor paper mill. He was thirty-two when he was demobbed, in 1945, and came home to his wife and a young son he had not yet seen. The war having been won, his duty now was to his young family (two daughters were to ensue) and he hired on at the mill as a draftsman.

"He was paid as a draftsman," Ron says, "but he was doing much more than draftsman's work."

Booth designed small dams, and laid out logging roads. He built the Windsor curling club. He won an award for design innovations related to specialized machinery used in the pulp and paper industry. He might have been skilled, imaginative, and resourceful, but without an engineering degree, Alec remained a draftsman until, one day, he cleaned out his office desk and went home to tell his wife that he had quit work. Their kids were grown, the two of them were adequately provided for, his duty to family was done.

"When my father started to work, the mill belonged to the Canada Paper Company. It was then bought by Howard Smith before changing hands again and becoming Domtar. At this point, they were bringing in new methods and my father recognized it was a good time to quit. He travelled for a year, wrote poetry, grew a beard. He was almost unrecognizable," Ron says.

But Windsor was home and it wasn't as if Booth's sudden retirement had gone unnoticed. He came home and considered some of the job offers which had come to him. He joined a major consulting firm in Toronto and, ironically, his first job was to help with the design and installation of a new Domtar mill. He suddenly found himself giving orders to the very same people who, just the year before, had been his superiors. He also worked for several years in a senior position with the Kruger Pulp & Paper mill in Bromptonville before taking a final retirement from engineering.

"I remember my father as a very good athlete," Ron recalls. "I was a good runner when I was young and I used to come home with ribbons and trophies from track meets. Well, when I was sixteen or seventeen, we all went on a holiday to a beach in Virginia. My dad challenged me to a race on the hard-packed sand and he blew right by me, left me in the dust," Ron laughs.

Booth was occasionally a speech writer for local politicians and also a land speculator. He purchased one hundred and eighty acres of what was mostly woodland at the edge of the town, cut most of the trees for pulp, and subdivided the land into building lots. The subdivision he planned enjoys both very spacious lots and wide streets—characteristics that initially displeased the town planning committee, but which those who live on the streets off Crabtree today quite cherish. (Booth is the shortest street in the subdivision; Crabtree the longest. Both are eponymous.)

The woman Booth married, Rita Codère, was an active, forceful, and very successful individual in her own right.

"She was very involved with the Liberals, both at the provincial and federal levels," Ron recalls. "We had René Levesque in our house more than once during the time that he was in the Liberal government of Jean Lesage. She was a tremendous organizer and was largely responsible for the surprise victory of Tobin [Asselin] over the Social Credit incumbent in the early '60s."

(In the general election of 1963, Joseph Patrick Tobin Asselin of Bromptonville stepped in to replace the Liberal candidate who had withdrawn less than a month before election day. To the surprise of the *Union Nationale* candidate, Asselin won the race by a few hundred votes.)

Ron's parents spent their last days at the Wales Home.

Alec Crabtree Booth was born in 1913 and passed away in 1997.

Post Office. The corner of Carpenter and Main Streets as it looked in the late 1940s. The Post Office was torn down in the early 1960s and replaced by a more modest brick building that now houses a pharmacy.
(RCHS Archival Collection)

# CHAPTER 21

# Who Was Johnny O. Toole?

NO DOUBT THERE ARE PRECEDENTS for the unusual gravestone in St. Andrew's Cemetery in Melbourne. It's easy to imagine, for example, that Samuel Langhorne Clemens has the name Mark Twain engraved on his tombstone. Still, it's not a frequent occurrence and that's what makes the final resting place of Johnny O. Toole rather exceptional; the granite marker that indicates his grave carries two names.

"When he passed away," says Bill Trippear of his father, "I wanted to have the name Johnny O. Toole on the gravestone because that's the name so many people knew him by. Hardly anybody knew Basil Trippear, but everyone knew Johnny O. Toole."

If you're fifty or older and grew up in the Richmond area, and if you were at all interested in country music, chances are you've heard the name, Johnny O. Toole. If so, you might also be aware of his legacy—a love of music that he passed on, not only to his own children, but to several others of his children's generation who learned to play the guitar from a man who is remembered as never being without a guitar in his hands.

"I don't know if anyone knows the origins of the name Johnny O. Toole," says Sydney Mills, who is married to Donna

Trippear, the oldest of Johnny O. Toole's four musical children. "Was it a name that he adopted for some reason, or did someone else name him that, I don't know. But everybody knew him by that name. I had been dating Donna for two years before I realized that Johnny O. Toole was a nickname and that the man who became my father-in-law was really named Basil Trippear."

(The name is even more enigmatic: on the gravestone it's written as Johnny O. Toole—an echo perhaps of Johnny B. Goode—but when spoken aloud the name sounds like Johnny O'Toole—like the actor, Peter O'Toole.)

"The phrase I remember is, 'Johnny O. Toole, the musical fool,' which seems a little unkind now but that moniker reflected the fact that he wasn't always an easy man," continues Sydney, a musician in his own right. "He didn't have an easy childhood and that marked him for life."

Eddy Campbelton, who was Basil Trippear's brother-in-law, recalls going to the Trippear house to see his sister, niece and nephews, and frequently seeing Johnny O. Toole sitting on the steps playing guitar. He echoes Sydney's words: "He was an odd fellow in some ways, as if there was a bit of an edge to him. He was a quiet man, not a talker. Sometimes he'd say hi, and other times he'd just keep picking his guitar and not say a word."

Basil Trippear was born in England on March 6, 1914, just a few months before the outbreak of the World War I. He was one of a number of siblings and even though the exact details are murky, the Trippear family circumstances must have been difficult because, at an early age, Basil was put into a foster home. In the summer of 1929, when he was fifteen, he was put on a ship with hundreds of other children and adolescents known as Home Children and sent to Canada. The luck of the draw had him end up in Melbourne, which was one of the centres that housed Home Children until they could be placed with particular families.

The lot of Home Children wasn't necessarily the easiest. Often, they were placed with farm families who were less interested in helping a homeless child than they were in acquiring an extra, unpaid farmhand.

In Basil Trippear's case, he ended up being sent to the Robinson farm in Melbourne, at the time one of the largest and most prosperous farms in the area. (The farm originally belonged to Daniel Thomas.)

"My father worked on the Robinson farm," says Sydney, "and my father remembered Basil Trippear for a very good reason. Basil was one of two Home Boys taken on by the farm. One winter day the two of them were sent out to shovel the manure from the pile into the spreader. The manure pile was frozen and the two boys realized that manure forks weren't a match for the frozen pile. At the time, dynamite was still relatively unregulated and farmers might have a few sticks around to deal with difficult tree stumps or inconvenient boulders. The boys found a stick of dynamite, worked it into the manure pile and lit the fuse."

Remarkably, despite the messy result, they remained employees at the farm.

It's not clear how long Trippear worked on the Robinson farm, but he also worked on the John Stott farm on what is now the Grainger Road. Mickey Blemings, who has fond childhood memories of Johnny O. Toole, recalls hearing that when he asked John Stott for a job on his farm, the young Englishman was willing to work for tobacco money and the washing of his clothes. It was the 1930s; the Depression was taking its toll, and he wasn't the only one who was working for little more than room and board.

Still, Trippear kept body and soul together, and ten years after arriving in Melbourne as a Home Boy, he returned to England as a soldier with the Canadian Heavy Artillery. It was 1939, World War II had broken out and, like many other young men, Trippear had been quick to enlist. He survived the war, returned to Melbourne, and, in June of 1947 married Beverley Campbelton, who for her part had served with the Women's Army Corps. The couple would soon have four children: Donna, Bill, Kent, and Raymond.

As a war veteran, Trippear's job prospects improved. He and his new wife had settled into a small house on the corner of what is now Route 243 and Cemetery Road, just below the Robinson farm where he had worked as a teenager. The house, which is still standing and still in the Trippear family, stood immediately adjacent to the house in which Frederick Coburn was born. His neighbour across the street, George Lovett (who was a close friend of Coburn) had a senior position with the Canadian National Railway and offered him a job as a call boy. The job (which had cost young Wilfrid Audet his life back in 1905) would not last long. As the telephone became a common household convenience in the years following World War II, train crews could be called more quickly and more easily without having recourse to fleet-footed call boys. The job became obsolete, but Basil continued to work for the CN in other capacities until his retirement.

Donna remembers her father as something of a stay-at-home dad. "He was always there for us," she says. "In the winter he used to make a rink for us in the backyard. It must have been quite small but we loved it and he enjoyed it just as much as we did. He was very athletic; he liked to swim in the summer, and in the winter he'd bring us skiing on the big hill behind our house. He was very good with his hands and he often made toys for us, sometimes recuperating parts and pieces from toys someone else had thrown out. But mostly, it was music. Our mother played the piano, by ear, and our father played the guitar, although he also played the harmonica, a bit of banjo and sometimes he played the spoons."

Unlike most spoon players who will bounce the spoons off their knee, Johnny O. Toole kept the spoons in a raised hand and used a quick snap of the wrist to tap out a percussive beat.

"When I was nine," Donna continues, "he started teaching me guitar. He had a dobro guitar and that was what I learnt on, just by imitating him. He taught my three brothers much the same way as they grew older and big enough to hold a guitar. All four of us took to music although each in our own way. Kent, for example, when he was very young, would take out my mother's pots and pans and bang on those. Not surprisingly, he became a drummer. Billy gravitated towards the bass, and Raymond towards the banjo. All six of us, counting my mother at the piano, would gather in the living room and play for hours."

On weekends, Johnny O. Toole was much in demand. Often this would be for a house party at which neighbours would gather on a Saturday night for several hours of socializing. Mickey Blemings, like Basil Trippear an army veteran (although twenty-five years younger), vividly remembers Johnny O. Toole.

"I was the youngest in my family," says Blemings, "and the only one who wasn't musical. My older brother was a good guitarist and my mother and sisters played the piano. On Saturday evenings, Johnny O. Toole would come over to our house, which stood where the small park now is, on the corner of Bridge Street and Melbourne Avenue. There would be a houseful of people and lots of music and Johnny O. Toole right in the middle of it with his guitar and his harmonica around his neck. He had a good voice too. I remember him singing songs like My Wild Irish Rose and old time Western songs by Gene Autry or Roy Rogers.

"My parents thought the world of Johnny O. Toole," he continues. "He didn't drink, certainly not more than an occasional beer. He didn't swear. He was very polite, and he was very kind. He was very kind to me. I remember him taking me in his old

Model A Ford to go swimming at Salmon Creek, or fishing higher up near the old dam on Salmon Creek. Maybe because he had had a difficult childhood himself, he was particularly attentive and kind towards children, and towards me.

"I was something of a street kid," Blemings recalls, "and sometimes we'd get into mischief. One of the games we liked to play was Hubcap, and we often played it on Cemetery Road just behind the Trippear house. Hubcaps had some value in the 1950s. We'd get a hubcap somewhere, and put it near the edge of the road, so it was easily visible to a driver. We'd have a long string tied to the hubcap and covered with a bit of gravel, and we'd have the other end of the string in our hands. We'd be hiding just off the road. When someone stopped to pick up the hubcap, we'd tug on the string and watch the motorist jump. I remember Beverly Trippear coming out her back door and watching us and laughing along with us. One night, a carload of older teenage boys managed to almost sneak up on us. If it hadn't been for the glow of their cigarettes and a bit of noise they made we might have been caught. As it was, we jumped up and ran like the dickens almost to the river to get away.

"The last time I saw him," Blemings continues, "was several years before he passed away. I was in Melbourne, with my son who was perhaps six or seven at the time. We'd been to see someone else in the neighbourhood and on a whim I thought I'd drop in on Johnny O. Toole. He was home and when I mentioned my name his face lit up. A few minutes later, one of his sons came in and the two of them took out guitar and banjo and set to playing."

While it didn't necessarily happen often, Johnny O. Toole sometimes played for a dance organized at one of the local halls and he would earn a few dollars for his evening's work.

"The first time I played for money," Donna recalls, "was at Gallup Hill. I was twelve years old, and I played with my dad and earned six dollars. I remember that the guitar I had wasn't much of an instrument with the strings too far from the fret board. My fingers were aching but I wasn't about to give up."

Later on, in the early 1970s, Donna, Bill, and Kent formed The Moonshiners and played locally for several years, carrying on their father's legacy. Similarly, Dennis Keenan, Bob Dunn, and Elwin Willey were taught to play by Johnny O. Toole and went on to perform locally.

"They would come to the house and sit in the front room and play," Kent Trippear recalls. "My father played entirely by ear and that's the way he taught others to play. He was patient and had a way of explaining things so they made sense; he had a way of boosting you along. He played country music; he liked Merle Haggard and Buck Owens. If he heard a song on the radio, he'd pick up the tune right away."

The lyrics were sometimes a different matter. Kent continues, "I remember one song in particular, Truck Driving Man it was called. Dad heard it on the radio and liked it and wanted to learn it. We had a reel-to-reel tape recorder and a hand held microphone. Dad finally managed to tape it off the radio and then he sat down, starting and stopping the tape recorder, to write down the words three or four at a time. But the next weekend, he was playing and singing the song as if he'd known it all his life."

Kent recalls having had a relatively strict upbringing. "Dad kept us on the straight and narrow," he says. "There was no alcohol in the house. We were taught to be polite and respectful. We really weren't allowed to go out until we were into our late teens. We were given lots of room to run and play but our parents always kept a close watch over us."

Bill points out that just as Johnny O. Toole shared his joy of music with a younger generation, he also shared his enthusiasm for athletic activity. "He taught us all how to swim," says Bill, "and a number of others as well. I remember a man by the name of Lawrence Henderson who went through the war. He often told me that he owed his life to dad because it was dad who had taught him to swim.

"He also loved to shoot," Bill says. "He wasn't a hunter so much as a target shooter. There was an old shed and I remember him shooting the door right off the shed. He was very upset when the gun laws changed in the 1960s and guns had to be licensed and restrictions were imposed on gun use."

"Maybe it was his experience with heavy artillery," says Kent, "but he liked explosions. I remember being quite small and we were in the yard setting off firecrackers. He saw us playing and thought we might want a little more excitement. He came back with dynamite caps, which you could still easily buy in those days. We set those off and we made a lot more noise than we had with the firecrackers."

Basil Trippear's final years were more difficult. He was frequently in and out of the hospital. He died of emphysema on June 9, 1986, at the age of seventy-two. His final resting place is in St. Andrew's Cemetery, at the top of the hill that overlooks the small house, at the bottom of the same hill, where he lived most of his life.

# PART 5

# TWENTY-FIRST-CENTURY ECHOES

Richmond's recorded history begins with the arrival of Americanized Europeans, descendants of British subjects fleeing religious persecution, now economic refugees of a newly minted Republic. The river brought them and helped sustain them. They settled on densely forested land and, for a while at least, lived to some extent on what they could hunt or trap. The forest, despite the fact that it yielded moose, rabbit, and partridge for the supper meal, was an antagonist to be laid low to make way for fields and pastures. The first colonists were almost entirely self-reliant. They lived in a wilderness that they saw as largely hostile.

By contrast, even if today we live in the countryside in refurbished nineteenth-century farmhouses a few kilometres from the nearest neighbour, we are urbanized and almost totally dependent on a socio-economic structure of which we are a minuscule part and of which we understand but little. We are rarely self-reliant.

Yet, the river still flows. Forests still stand. Wildlife is still to be found. Our relationship today to the world around us can occasionally evoke unexpected echoes of what has changed and what has not.

# CHAPTER 22

# Jacques and the River

Anyone who glanced at the St. Francis River in the summer of 2012 noticed how very low the river was. Towards the end of August, people crossing Richmond's Mackenzie Bridge noticed not only half a dozen large sandbars of which they had never before been aware, but also several discarded tires which someone with artistic aspirations had stood upright on some of the sandbars.

"It bothered me to see those tires," says Jacques Thibeault whose home in Melbourne Township is a riverfront property. For a week or more, every time he crossed the bridge he noticed them, until finally, on the morning of Saturday, September 1, Thibeault climbed into his canoe and set off to do something about the tires. What he expected to be a morning's work stretched on for four full days.

"I ended up finding lots of things in the river," he says. "I fished out four bicycles, a road sign or two, as well as the tub and transmission of an old washing machine. But for the most part, it was tires I picked up, one hundred and twenty-five in all. The biggest was a tire from some sort of loader; it was a good four feet high. There were whitewall tires that had probably been in the river for half a century or more because tires with white sidewalls were popular in the 1950s and 1960s. There were narrow, large-diameter tires that date back to the 1930s or 1940s."

Fishing them out was no easy task. "Old tires stink," he affirms. "They smell pretty bad after that long in the river. Worse, the rubber has deteriorated so that sometimes the tire starts to come apart in your hands.

"The task was straight forward," Thibeault explains. "I'd set off in my canoe and when I got to a tire, I would climb out of the canoe, loop a rope attached to the canoe around my left arm so as to not lose the canoe, and then I'd tackle the tire. I'd wash it somewhat to try and get most of the sand out. Sometimes I'd find a crayfish that had taken up residence. I would then tip the tire into the canoe and go on to the next one.

"Between canoe trips, I'd go to the bridges to spot the tires," he continues. "They're much easier to see from higher up. I'd make a quick sketch to remind me where they were and then I'd go back to my canoe and get another load. I could put anywhere from six to ten tires in the canoe at one time, depending on their size, because there were truck tires as well as car tires. When the canoe was full I paddled to the east bank and unloaded my cargo. I made a first pile of old tires near the Nautical Park and then I made two more piles near the Coburn Bridge."

Over the four days that he spent collecting tires, the canoe enthusiast paddled the mile or so of the Richmond riverfront some fifteen times or more. "Tires are heavy so they settle to the bottom. For the most part they were along the east bank (the Richmond side of the river as opposed to the Melbourne side) or in the middle of the river. The biggest thing I noticed on the river bottom was a long piece of structural steel which at one time must have been part of the Mackenzie Bridge. I'm going to call the transport ministry because it's undoubtedly theirs. It won't be easy to fish out but it really should be picked up," he says.

"I had the help of several other people," Thibeault adds. "As I was piling some tires on the river bank near the Nautical Park, I saw Myriam Beaulieu, one of the park employees. When she learned what I was doing, she was keen on helping out."

Myriam was joined by her sister, Roxane, and her friend Mathieu Rheault, as well as Jacques' friends, Marie-Ève Trottier and François Daigle. Together they transported four trailer-loads of tires from the riverbank to a storage site belonging to the Town of Richmond, where they are now waiting to leave for their final destination, a recycling site.

"The Town of Richmond was helpful," Jacques notes. "They lent us a trailer and found a place to store the tires temporarily. They have also undertaken to contact a recycler.

"I suppose I did this because I saw that it was something that needed doing and I happened to have a bit of time," he shrugs. "I see it as a gesture towards righting a historical wrong. Some of those old tires are relics from the beginning of consumerism. In the 1950s and 1960s, the river was still being used as a dump site. People threw their garbage into the river and the current washed it away.

"It was also possible to do because the river has never been so low and that made it easy to find and pick up a lot of this junk," he says.

"I cleaned up a small stretch of the river," he continues, "though probably one of the worst parts because it's flowing through an urban area, but there's a lot more river to clean, I'm sure. I know that there are places upstream that are quite littered."

This is not the first time that Thibeault has put his beliefs into practice. Last summer, he spent a few days cleaning several hundred feet of his riverfront and that of a neighbouring property. At that time, among much other debris, he found sizable pieces of metal that were recognizably remnants of fenders of old cars.

While Jacques Thibeault acted spontaneously and independently, he is not alone in taking steps to make our rivers cleaner. For the last twenty years, Action Saint-François in Sherbrooke has been organizing crews of volunteers who, among other things, donate their time to clean riverbanks in the St. Francis River Basin.

# CHAPTER 23

# The Last Trapper

In the twenty-first century, trappers are rarely seen in a positive light, even though trapping—at least in the Eastern Townships—is most often carried out in order to remove a wild animal that has become a nuisance or is posing a potential danger. That's the experience of Raymond Fortier, who is both a lifetime trapper and a long-serving Melbourne Township councillor.

"Last summer, I was trapping near the bike path," Fortier recalls. "A farmer had noticed that beavers had moved in and the dam they were building was going to eventually flood one of his fields. The farmer called the municipality and I was asked to remove them. Some people riding by didn't much like what I was doing and they told me that wild animals have a right to live, that there are very few beavers left, that I shouldn't be trapping. It was hard to explain.

"Of course, they were wrong about beavers," he continues. "There are lots of them around and they can do considerable damage. Not long ago, I was called to the Spooner Pond Road. Beavers had started building a dam in a ditch along the road. In the end, I trapped nine of them. Then I had to take apart the dam they'd built. No easy task because each stick has to come out one at a time. It's a long, hard job. It also gives you a real appreciation for their engineering skills."

Human engineering eventually outwitted beaver engineering on the Gee Road, which connects Highway 143 to Highway 116. A good stretch of the gravel road runs through Gore swamp before joining the 116 near the spot where a small train station once stood.

"The Gee Road has cost the Municipality of Melbourne more than a few truckloads of gravel because of beavers," Fortier says. "This was several years ago. It was October and I came back from a hunting vacation to learn that Jason Badger, who maintains our roads, had been trying to call me all week. Beavers had blocked a four-foot culvert near the Gore railway crossing and the road was on the point of being washed out. It was especially difficult—and dangerous—to take that dam apart because the beavers had built it in the culvert.

"But we haven't had problems since then," he continues, "because the municipality installed a simple, but effective mechanism. Picture a series of vertical posts that slide into a cement base. The beavers use the posts to start building their dam by weaving lengths of wood between the vertical posts. When we notice this happening, we lift out the posts and the dam loses its strength and collapses. After this happens two or three times, the beavers move somewhere else."

Trapping is something Fortier can't explain. "It's in the blood," he says. "In my case, it was from my mother. She grew up in Delson on the banks of the St. Lawrence. She went trapping for muskrat with her older brothers. They'd bring their catch to the Bonsecours market in Old Montreal and sell the entire animal for twenty-five cents.

"I started trapping woodchucks in the fields behind the house when I was a youngster," Fortier continues, "and in 1971 I bought my first license. It was for muskrat, which I trapped

Cooling off, circa 1930. The St. Francis and its tributaries offered
any number of swimming holes where kids could spend a summer afternoon.
That two boys are wearing ties suggests this group may have detoured
by the river on their way home from school.
(Courtesy of Bob Laberge)

along the St. Francis. I caught twenty-four that year. When the
pelts were sold at auction later in the spring, I got one dollar
and thirty-one cents per pelt—minus the commission."

He still traps muskrat, but no longer on the St. Francis. "The
river has gotten much lower," he observes. "Places where I used
to go swimming as a boy, where the water was six feet deep, are
now so shallow that you can almost walk across without getting
your feet wet. The river no longer rises in the spring as it once
did. Muskrat season runs from the end of March to the twenty-
first of April. It used to be that the river would be high for a
good three weeks or more; now we might get high water for a
week if we're lucky. By the time you've set your traps, you've got
to take them in.

"You depend on high water to trap muskrat," Fortier explains.
"My traps essentially consist of a board and a short cedar post

on which I set my trap and a couple of carrots, one above and one below the trap, for bait. Muskrats are swimming up and down the river. They'll climb on the board to rest, notice the carrots, get the first one, and then step into the trap as they go for the second one."

Over the last forty years, Fortier has turned his hand to trapping a surprisingly wide variety of wildlife. "Last year I sent in over a hundred pelts: Two coyote, two fox, three fisher, twelve mink, forty-seven beaver, and seventy-three muskrat. But I've also trapped otter, which I've found both in the St. Francis and in some of its tributaries. I caught a bobcat as well last year, though it was an accidental catch. I've also found herons in muskrat traps; the birds weren't harmed by the trap but liberating the birds was surprisingly dangerous because of their beaks."

Accidental catches are brought to game wardens in Sherbrooke. Bobcats are relatively rare, though there were eighty-four accidental catches of bobcat in 2011, a sufficiently high number that, in 2012, for the first time in several years, licenses to trap bobcat were issued for the period from mid-November to mid-December.

Fortier's pelts are collected twice a year, in January and again in April, by an agent of the Fur Harvesters Auction, and brought to North Bay where, five times a year, tens and even hundreds of thousands of pelts are auctioned at sales which can span two days. Buyers are couturières and manufacturers who come primarily from across North America and Europe. Despite anti-fur campaigns that have been mounted in recent years, in 2011, Fur Harvesters had the highest gross sales since their inception in 1947.

With pelts collected but twice a year, Fortier sometimes finds himself having to wait several months before the next pick up. "I have my own freezer," he says. "If need be, I put my catch there. I always have some beaver in the freezer because beaver flesh is what I use to bait my traps. Except for muskrat and beaver, most of the animals I trap for their pelts are carnivores."

Fortier estimates that seventy percent of his trapping is related to nuisance animals. "I've saved the municipalities of Melbourne, Cleveland and Ulverton quite a bit of money over the years if you think of the cost of rebuilding a washed-out road," he says. "Besides beavers, the other common nuisance animals are raccoons and skunks."

Fortier most often uses Conibear traps, which kill the trapped animal instantly, but he also uses box traps that capture the animal without killing or physically harming it. "Imagine a box with a screen at one end and a cone-like opening at the other. The bait is placed at the screen end. The animal smells and sees the bait but has to go through the cone end to get the bait. Once in, it can't get out.

"Catching skunks," he warns, "can be a little smelly. I've been sprayed once or twice. The trick is to get a heavy cloth over the box. The skunk won't spray if it's in a dark, enclosed space. Once the skunk is wrapped up like that, it's easy to pick up the box and move it. On average, I probably catch and release about twenty skunks per year, and I'm usually called because the animal is digging up a well-manicured lawn looking for grubs. People also call for raccoons that are getting into gardens or garbage."

Raymond Fortier belongs to the Fédération des trappeurs gestionnaires du Québec, an organization that has about two hundred and fifty members in the Townships. "There are also people trapping who do not belong to the organization," he warns, "but despite the trapping we do, wildlife numbers in the area are stable, and there are some populations that are on the rise."

# CHAPTER 24

# The New Age Forester

EVERY SPRING, since 2005, the Groupement Forestier Coopératif Saint-François has been giving an annual award to a woodlot owner who has taken exemplary care of his or her woodlot. Typically the winner might be expected to be a very fit and very energetic lumberjack aged somewhere between his late thirties and early fifties.

In 2013, that stereotype was well off the mark.

Anita Mercier Demers, who won the "forester emeritus" that year, is a rather diminutive, cheery nonagenarian who has never operated a chain saw in her life.

"I've used an axe and a brush saw and a few other tools in the woods, but never a chain saw," says the South Durham native who is a long-time Richmond resident.

"The truth is, I felt a little embarrassed when I found out I was getting the award," she says. "I don't deserve it. Really, it should have gone to my son-in-law, Claude. He's the one who has been doing most of the heavy lifting for quite a while now. The award was given to me only because the land is in my name."

Still, when asked when she'd last been in her one hundred and fifteen-acre woodlot to work, she replied, "Just last fall. I helped out by holding steady the branches that my son-in-law, was cutting up into lengths and by cording the firewood."

One of six children born on a rural property on the McGivney Road in South Durham, Anita grew up with two great loves, that of music and the woods. "My father, who was originally from the States, worked for the railroad," she says, "but he didn't want his children to grow up in the city. It wasn't possible for my father to work on the trains and to farm, but we grew up with fields and forests around us and, as a child, I was often off exploring the woods with two of my brothers."

The daughter of a railroad man, she married into railroad life and lived in several different places—including Morrisburg, Ontario, and Cantic, on the American border—before coming to Richmond in 1957 when her husband, Gérard Demers, was appointed Stationmaster here.

"My husband was from Lisgar, which was once one of the two stops between Richmond and South Durham on the milk run," Anita says. "He loved being in the woods, just as I do. He was also a hunter. I tried hunting but the one time I shot a rabbit, I burst into tears, so I knew it wasn't for me. A decade after we moved here, we bought a small property with a chalet just at the edge of town. Originally, we were co-owners with a friend. Eventually we bought his share and we've owned the property ever since. Although the first piece of land was quite small, we were able to add to it when two adjacent owners sold us their properties.

"We bought the extra land," she explains, "because we wanted to be sure to have a quiet, restful space around our chalet.

"We've never really exploited our woodlot," Anita says. "It's always been a little haven for our family. My husband and I always got so much pleasure out of the woodlot. It's been just as wonderful for our daughters, Hélène and Suzanne, and for our five grandchildren and our eight great-grandchildren."

From the beginning, the woodlot was also the site of a good deal of hard work. Half a century ago, the Demers property looked far different, being the site of a couple of small, abandoned, gravel pits and the Town garbage dump. Today, there is no sign of the earlier activities, and the land is covered by a well-maintained, mixed forest, unscarred save for fifteen kilometres of trails. These are used by the family all-terrain vehicle in the summer and provide venues for cross-country skiing and snowshoeing in the winter. "I stopped skiing five years ago," Anita admits, "but I still snowshoe.

"At the beginning we had an old tractor," says Anita, "which my husband used to haul deadfalls out of the woods. We never heated with wood ourselves, so the firewood we cut was given to friends. We also planted nine thousand trees. We would drive to East Angus to pick up seedlings, then come home and put them in the ground."

In 1991, two years after the death of her husband, Anita joined the Groupement Forestier Coopératif Saint-François, an organization that can help woodlot owners with all the steps involved in caring for a forest, from planting trees to supervising their harvesting.

Since 1991, she has had another twenty thousand trees planted: softwoods like white pine, red pine, black spruce, and tamarack, but also hardwoods like ash and red oak. With help from the Groupement she has had underbrush cleared, drainage ditches dug, thinning carried out, and more trails made.

The transformation of the Demers woodlot, from before to after, is not quite as dramatic as the change portrayed in the award-winning, animated film, *The Man Who Planted Trees*, but it's not far off the mark.

As a youngster growing up, Anita's two great passions were music and the outdoors. If her woodlot satisfied the latter, the former was served, at least in part, by Les Amis de la Musique and the Centre d'Art de Richmond, with which she was very much involved for a quarter century. She sat on the board of directors for many years and was also a long-time member of the committee that looked after booking artists for concerts. It was a rare concert at which Anita would not be working as a volunteer at the ticket booth or at the bar during intermission.

"I only ever learnt the piano," she says, "and I never became more than competent enough to play for family and friends, but—just like the outdoors—music has always been very important to me. I'm doubly blessed because both of my daughters share my love of nature and of music. Both are very accomplished at the piano."

Besides playing the piano, Anita has always loved to sing. Today she is still part of St. Bibiane's parish choir. Previously, in 1973, as part of the Estria Choir, she sang in Edmonton and, in 1975, as part of the Choralies Internationales, had the experience of participating in a project which saw singers from several different countries spend a week on a Russian passenger ship, the Alexander Pushkin, where they practiced daily and mounted a concert at the end of the week.

Anita still sits on the board of directors of the Centre d'action bénévole de Richmond and continues to serve as a driver for the Meals on Wheels program.

What's next for Richmond's award-winning, nonagenarian forester?

It would seem more work in the woods. Even as she sat down for this short interview, she was interrupted twice by phone calls, and both had to do with upcoming projects this spring on her award-winning property.

PART 6

# FACING THE FUTURE

DESPITE WHAT WE MIGHT READ in the astrology columns and in Nostradamus, our best indicator of what the future might bring would seem to come either from past experience or from the song Che sarà sarà. The number is ever smaller but there are still people who annually buy a Farmers' Almanac to know what the coming year will bring. In 2016, the term post-truth was coined to describe our era. In the post-truth era, what is true can just as easily be determined by an emotional reaction as it can be by an analysis of facts. A population, affected by emotion, will determine something to be true, even if the facts would irrefutably indicate otherwise. One question facing us all is: what is true?

CHAPTER 25

# Flirting with Fluoridation

O N FEBRUARY 1, 2016, the Richmond Town Council approved
a payment of one hundred and twenty-seven thousand, one
hundred and fifty-two dollars to the Ministry of Health and
Social Services, and so closed the books—for a second time—on
water fluoridation in Richmond. The sum (two per cent of the
Town's budget that year) represented fifty percent of the costs
incurred five years earlier when Richmond started fluoridating
its water. The fluoridation installations and some upgrading to
the pumping station had cost Richmond nothing; the provincial
government had covered all costs. The payment to the Ministry
in 2016 was not for service provided; rather, it was a penalty
imposed on the Town for ceasing water fluoridation.

For the people of Richmond (and a few dozen households in
Cleveland and Melbourne connected to Town water), that sum
was the price paid for an introduction to both a complex chemical quandary and an exercise in participatory democracy.

Richmond's saga with water fluoridation has been repeated
tens of thousands of times across North America, although not
many towns have gone through the exercise twice.

The concept of water fluoridation began with an observation made by a scientifically-minded American dentist. After retiring from a career as a dentist that spanned three decades in the same location in Colorado, Dr. F.S. McKay published a paper in 1916 on what was then called mottled enamel. In analysing his patients' records, he noticed a high incidence of what we now call dental fluorosis: teeth permanently marked by white, yellow, or brown stains. McKay postulated that mottled enamel was caused by something in the water. He also made a secondary observation: his patients had a slightly lower incidence of cavities, or dental caries, than would have been expected.

Fifteen years later, the United States Public Health Services (USPHS) identified McKay's toxic agent as fluoride (in layman's terms, a variant of the fluorine element carrying an extra electrical charge). Fluoride has no colour, smell, or taste, and so is undetectable to our senses, not unlike other trace elements in our water. The Health Service research showed that 0.6 parts per million caused mild but detectable dental fluorosis in a small percentage of the population, but at fluoride concentrations of 2.0 ppm, the incidence of fluorosis became an acute and urgent public health problem.

During the mid-1930s, a number of communities in the United States started treating their water supply to remove fluoride with the intention of eliminating dental fluorosis. While dental fluorosis doesn't pose any serious health risks, it can cause a quite noticeable disfigurement. There is no "cure" for dental fluorosis and the only way to hide it is through the relatively expensive procedure of capping the affected teeth. Removing fluoride from drinking water seemed a sensible solution.

However, before long, another scientist, G.J. Cox, a biochemist in dental research working in Pittsburgh at the Mellon Institute of Industrial Research (which has since become the Mellon Carnegie University), was promoting a radically different view of fluoridated water. Cox, pointing to McKay's observation that fluoride in water resulted in fewer cavities, advocated adding fluoride to water where it did not occur naturally.

It is significant that Cox was involved with industrial research.

Edward Groth, in a doctoral thesis entitled "Two Issues of Public Policy," points out that in the years following World War II, there were political reasons to portray fluoride as beneficial. Farmers, who had seen their crops and orchards destroyed by air-borne pollutants, notably fluorides, emanating from war-time factories, were asking for financial compensation from the government of the United States. If the U.S. Government was found to be liable for turning profitable agricultural land toxic, and rendering prosperous farmers poor, so too was Industrial America.

The USPHS determined that at a concentration of one part per million, naturally fluoridated water resulted in sixty percent fewer cavities while affecting ten percent of the same population with the mildest forms of dental fluorosis. In terms of public health, the USPHS judged this outcome to be acceptable and one part per million was set as the standard for allowable fluoride concentration. (It has since been lowered to 0.6 ppm.) But the Health Service was cognizant of possible secondary effects of fluoridated water: mottled enamel and, in extreme cases, skeletal deformation, so that when the idea of adding fluoride to drinking water was first proposed, the USPHS took a neutral stance, neither endorsing nor discouraging the practice.

Water fluoridation began in Wisconsin in the early 1940s and, by mid-century, there were more towns and cities fluoridating water in Wisconsin (fifty) than in the rest of the United States combined (forty-seven). The means by which certain communities came to have fluoridated water, and others did not, became a pattern that endures even today.

Proponents of water fluoridation took speaking engagements all over the state, addressing Parent-Teacher Associations, women's clubs, and civic groups. They organized political campaigns to persuade local officials to approve of fluoridation. Even though evidence in favour of fluoridation was not as strong as it might have been, their tactic was to discredit objections of those opposed to fluoridation and, in the interest of political expediency, to never admit the possibility of doubt or disagreement over scientific evidence. Their tactics included personal attacks on those who opposed fluoridation for any reason. They didn't restrict themselves to scientific debate, but rather pushed fluoridation into the political realm.

The move towards fluoridating water was largely based on lobbying and the first target was the medical establishment. By the end of the 1940s, any number of professional associations (American Institute of Nutrition, American Association of Industrial Dentists, American Academy of Paediatrics) including the USPHS had declared themselves in support of fluoridation.

Still, there was a backlash. By the 1950s, in many communities, the proponents of fluoridation were met by local, grassroots opponents who were often able to organize effective political campaigns and force a referendum. In most cases, if fluoridation was brought to a civic referendum, it was defeated. If citizens didn't organize themselves to protest, they found themselves with fluoridated water.

"Experts on both sides of this issue," Groth wrote, "have shown a tendency to cite evidence selectively, ignoring, or dismissing as not valid, data that do not support their argument. Proponents and opponents alike have been very uncritical in accepting as valid that evidence which matches the policy position they wish to promote, and have been highly critical of, and attempted to find all potential flaws which might invalidate, any research that has implications contrary to those desired."

After seven decades, water fluoridation remains controversial. The pattern of lobbyists facing off against grass-roots opponents is similarly well established.

Richmond's first encounter with fluoridation came in the mid-1970s, and it was a low-key affair. "I can't provide exact dates off the top of my head," says André Lupien, who became a town councillor in 1967 before being acclaimed as mayor in 1974, a position he held until he retired from politics in 1986. "I do remember that the Liberal provincial government at the time, under Robert Bourassa, had embarked on a plan to have all of Quebec drinking fluoridated water. I do know that not a single citizen in Richmond asked for water fluoridation and that no one complained when we ceased fluoridation.

"I'm not a doctor and not a chemist," Lupien says, "so I knew little about it, but a chance encounter with Jean Drapeau, the mayor of Montreal, led me to question the wisdom of fluoridation. I was the mayor of a small town of thirty-five hundred, he was the mayor of what was then Canada's largest and most cosmopolitan city, so we didn't have that much in common. But one file we did share was water fluoridation.

"Drapeau was unequivocally against fluoridation," Richmond's ex-mayor continues. "He had access to well-educated, well-informed people. He defined fluoride as a deadly poison. It was a brief encounter but a memorable one."

Drapeau was not alone in his concerns. "I remember that adding fluoride to our water weighed very heavily on Normand Cormier, the foreman of Richmond's public works crew. He was worried that he might make an error, or that something would malfunction. He had been given training in operating the fluoridation equipment, and he knew what he was doing, but he worried that something could go wrong."

He was concerned for good reasons. "The mechanism kept clogging," explains Normand Cormier. "Virtually every single day, we were spending time doing repairs or making adjustments on the mechanism.

"The fluoride salt," he continues, "was delivered like flour in big, one hundred-pound paper bags. The water, drawn from a well, was pumped to the reservoir through an eighteen-inch pipe. The fluoride salt was dumped into a large tub which had a small pipe, an inch or so in diameter, equipped with a screw mechanism, coming out of the bottom. The fluoride salt was supposed to be fed by the screw into the main water pipe."

The fact that the small pipe kept clogging and needed almost daily attention made fluoridation not just a medically questionable practice, but a relatively expensive maintenance issue as well.

Just as council meeting minutes from that time don't reveal when Richmond started fluoridating, so too do they not reveal exactly when fluoridation stopped.

What Cormier does remember is that the mayor came to the pumping station, looked at the bags, and gave the order to stop fluoridating. Over the next few months, during his spare time, Cormier himself dismantled the screw mechanism, the feed pipe, and the holding tub.

"Things were more relaxed in those days," says Lupien. "At some point I got a phone call from a provincial bureaucrat who wanted to know if we'd started fluoridating. I told him that we had stopped, that if Montreal started then we would start. I alarmed him when I told him that I intended to simply dispose of the bags of fluoride salt at the town dump. He told me that they absolutely must not be dumped. They had to be returned. I found it very curious that he wanted me to put fluoride salts in the town drinking water but those same salts were somehow too dangerous for the dump."

Some thirty-five years later, again under a business-friendly, provincial Liberal government (led by Jean Charest), the Ministry of Health and Social Services again embarked on a program to fluoridate drinking water across the province. This time, there was more involved than a phone call from a bureaucrat.

Richmond was one of the early targets of the fluoridation initiative, likely, at least in part, because of its status as an economically disadvantaged town.

Clifford Lancaster was a long-serving alderman on Richmond's Town Council. He recalls the decision to opt for fluoridation was not easily made. "We debated fluoridation at council for a whole year," he says, "and I personally don't really know if it's good or bad. We heard an awful lot and in the end we decided that the 'good' outweighed the 'bad' and we decided to go with it, especially since the provincial government was paying for all the installations."

Yet, when the announcement was made that Richmond was fluoridating its water, it was a surprise to almost everyone. While councillors may have debated fluoridation for a whole year, not one member of the council thought to discuss fluoridation with his constituents. And, despite those discussions, at least one councillor still had trouble wrapping his tongue around the word and referred to it as floration.

The news that Richmond was going to fluoridate its water evoked an angry reaction. People who never attended council meetings turned up to ask why there had been no consultation with the public. In June 2012, two years after the Town started fluoridating its water, a group formed under the name

Regroupement pour une eau saine à Richmond (Citizens for Healthy Water in Richmond) to fight fluoridation. Spearheaded by several young mothers including Marylène Prévost, Mandy Demers, and Ève-Marie Arcand (a dentist), the group formally requested that Richmond cease fluoridation.

In September of 2012, the Town organized an information meeting. Public Health officials agreed to speak, but not in the presence of the grass-roots group; they were willing to present their position, but not to debate it. A month later, the Regroupement presented the Town with a petition signed by over a thousand citizens demanding that water fluoridation cease. In December of 2012, bowing to the will of the population, Richmond formally requested permission to stop water fluoridation.

Richmond was not alone in contesting the provincial government's plan to have all of Quebec drinking fluoridated water. The issue was being hotly debated in Trois-Rivières, where the city council, in a split decision, voted in favour of fluoridation, as in Beaupré, where the city paid a forty-five thousand dollar penalty for stopping fluoridation.

Prompted in part by Karine Vallières, the Liberal Member of the National Assembly for the Richmond riding, who was responding to a request from the anti-fluoridation group, the provincial government held a Parliamentary Commission on water fluoridation at the end of April 2013. The Commissioners received over thirty dossiers and heard from almost a dozen groups, including the Regroupement from Richmond. A week later, it released its findings: the goal of fluoridating drinking water across the province should be maintained, but municipalities had to insure that the addition of fluoride was socially acceptable to its citizens.

The Commission's report was disappointing. Neither of the key questions raised by the Regroupement were addressed: if fluoride is a medication, is it ethical to mass medicate an entire population; why, as fluoride salt is an additive, are there no pharmacological tests on it?

The Parliamentary Commission left the Town in a quandary. Clearly, fluoridation was not socially acceptable to its citizens, but ceasing fluoridation at any time in the first five years would mean a penalty amounting to eighty percent of the installation costs. Where in its budget could the Town possibly find two hundred thousand dollars? Would Richmond's ratepayers accept a hike (albeit small) in taxes to pay the penalty?

The question played out six months later during the municipal elections held in November; fluoridation was very much an issue.

The mayor, Marc-André Martel, who was first elected in 1986, was returned by acclamation, but he found himself with four new councillors at the table. Whether fluoride was beneficial or not remained undecided, but there was unanimity in the new council that the townspeople of Richmond deserved to say whether or not they wanted to drink fluoridated water. There would have to be a referendum, or better yet, because it is far less expensive to administer, a public consultation. Whichever it was (the former being binding; the latter only a recommendation), the Town council promised to abide by the result. A public consultation would be held but when, and how would the question be worded?

The wording was easy: Are you in favour of ceasing fluoridation and the accompanying tax hike? Yes or no. The timing required more thought. For a segment of the population, it was imperative to stop fluoridating immediately. However, immediate cessation came with a penalty of over two hundred thousand dollars, whereas waiting a year would reduce the penalty to a little over one hundred and twenty-five thousand. Even staunch members of the Regroupement could see the wisdom of a later date for a public consultation, and it was eventually set for Sunday, October 19, 2014.

Both sides set out to win the hearts and the minds of Richmond's thirty-two hundred inhabitants. Public Health used public funds to mount an advertising campaign that featured full-page ads in the area's guaranteed-circulation weeklies. In April of 2014, Ministry officials in Sherbrooke issued a press release announcing that school-aged children in Richmond had been found to have three times fewer cavities since fluoridation started in 2010.

If the ads had annoyed members of the Regroupement, they found the news item infuriating. Letters to the editor decried it as false and misleading, as it was. The data (gathered by dental hygienists) may have been accurate (or not) but it in no way conformed to a structured scientific study. But for the Ministry, this was a propaganda war, and the Ministry bureaucrats were treating it as such.

If Public Health was carrying out blanket bombing raids, the Regroupement was engaged in guerrilla warfare. Aside from one small pamphlet (funding for which was raised by passing a hat), the group fighting fluoridation relied on word of mouth to present the case for clean water. Members of the group went door-to-door for a few hours every evening over a period of several months to present their case personally.

In mid-October, a week before the public consultation of October 19, a second public meeting was held, this time at the Centre d'Art de Richmond, and this time spokespeople for both sides were on the stage together. In keeping with their tactics, the Ministry brought several of their staff to the meeting. They were conspicuous by their dress (having come to the 7:00 pm meeting directly from work, they were still in their business suits) and by their behaviour, as they'd come, not to listen, but to distract by fidgeting and whispering whenever a speaker from the Regroupement had the floor.

Throughout the propaganda war and the public meetings, Ministry officials, while unflinchingly adamant about the benefits of fluoridation, were also unable or unwilling to give more than rote replies that failed to answer numerous questions. Since fluoride acts on the surface of the tooth, why drink it? Since only a small percentage of the water we use is actually consumed, why fluoridate all water? Why has Europe banned water fluoridation? How, without fluoridated water, does Europe have statistically healthier teeth? Why do we not adopt a European approach to dental health? Can the Ministry confirm or deny that the fluoride salts put in our drinking water come from industrial waste? Can the Ministry provide toxicology reports on the fluoride salts so citizens would know exactly what they are ingesting? What compensation will there be for those who develop dental fluorosis? What about newborns and infants, since the American Dental Association specifically warns against fluoride for the very young? Since there are as many scientific studies casting doubt on the benefits of fluoridation as there are studies promoting it, why not wait until there is definitive and unquestionable proof of its efficacy before imposing it?

Neither at the two public meetings, nor in the press, did Public Health officials address any of the many questions and criticisms regarding water fluoridation.

The Public Consultation on Fluoridation held on October 19, 2014 was something of an anticlimax. The result was unequivocal; seventy-six percent voted against water fluoridation even though it meant a household tax of fifty dollars a year for two years. More surprising was the voter turnout, a disappointing twenty-five percent. Only one in four eligible voters bothered to say yes or no to fluoridation.

In the bigger picture, perhaps the large non-voting majority was reflecting the fact that fluoride actually affects very few people. Even the most supportive studies on fluoridated water show that the practice provides a mere five percent reduction in cavities. (Other studies suggest fluoridation has no effect at all in reducing cavities.) Despite occasional claims that dental caries is reaching epidemic proportions, dental statistics show that the average person will have about ten cavities in his lifetime and filling a cavity is a simple, straightforward, and relatively inexpensive procedure.

So, why so much time, energy, money, and trickery devoted by government bureaucrats to water fluoridation when other measures (such as heavily taxing junk food) could potentially bring about much greater health benefits? The unstated answer seems to be that the fluoridation of drinking water—like the sale of junk food—is good for business if not for health.

CHAPTER 26

# The Last Word

AS WAS MENTIONED at the beginning of this book, in the summer of 2012, as part of its fiftieth anniversary celebrations, the Richmond County Historical Society interred a time vault under local artist Jean-Marc Tétreault's sculpted metal tree erected between the Melbourne Township Town Hall and the Melbourne Market.

The time vault turned out to be a surprisingly successful fundraising event for the Society. For fifty dollars, participants put items of their choosing in a small, hermetically sealed, kitchen canister that, on the afternoon of Sunday, September 2, was placed in a cement culvert, six feet underground. As a crowd collectively cheered, a backhoe gently laid a cement lid on the culvert and efficiently filled the hole with dirt. The Historical Society, with archival diligence, noted the names of those who had had their time capsules interred while the hundred or more people in attendance speculated as to who might or might not be around in 2062 to see the time vault unearthed and opened.

There was an element of whimsy to the time vault project, but it also spoke to deeper feelings of our own place in the trajectory of time, an acknowledgement that while we might reflect on our past, our beckoning mortality will delineate the extent of our future. What will not-so-distant descendants make of the pennies and paper clips and USB keys and a myriad of other small curiosities of our times so thoughtfully deposited in those canisters? For that matter, will there be descendants still in the area to move the statue, unearth the time vault, and open the canisters? What will the place that we call home be like fifty years from now? We may know a little about the past of the Richmond area but what about its future?

If experience of the past can be a predicator of the future, Richmond's longest-serving mayor is singularly well placed to look ahead and extrapolate. No mayor has served the Town longer than Marc-André Martel who has held the post for thirty-one years, almost a quarter of the Town's existence. In a three-way mayoral race in 1986, Martel took roughly two thirds of the vote, leaving the two other candidates, Marcel Gariépy and Nelson Murphy, to share the remaining third. With the exception of that first election, he has never campaigned for office, being returned to the mayor's chair by acclamation in all subsequent municipal elections.

To spend thirty-one uninterrupted years at the helm of a municipality is, of itself, a rarity. Even more unusual is that Martel began and ended his career in the mayor's chair. He didn't follow the usual path that normally sees a long-term municipal politician spend at least a short stint as a councillor.

Martel's road to Richmond and the mayor's chair was relatively short if not entirely direct. He was born and raised in Asbestos, only twenty minutes by car east of Richmond. He chose to study law and attended the University of Sherbrooke, approximately thirty minutes by car south of Richmond. It was a work placement session during his Law studies that brought him to Richmond. Even at the time, he considered it a lucky break.

"I was placed with Georges Savoie, who had a law practice in Richmond at the time, and who went on to become a judge," Martel recalls. "Despite the fact that he was practicing in a small town, he had an exceptional legal library, largely because he had inherited or acquired the library of Gaston Desmarais, a son of Stanislas-Edmond Desmarais and a Richmond lawyer who had also gone on to become a judge. For me, as a student, it was an exceptional opportunity. This, of course, was long before the days of the Internet and instant access to almost everything.

"I got a summer job with Georges Savoie when I was in my third year of Law," he recalls, "and my salary was fifty dollars a week."

Still, in 1971, not long after passing his bar exam—at the time, an arduous, two-day affair at McGill University that roughly three out of ten applicants failed to pass—he was approached by George Savoie. The older lawyer was moving to Sherbrooke and was selling his practice in Richmond. Was Marc-André interested?

"It was an extensive practice," Martel recalls. "For the first three or four years, I was working seven days a week. I took my first vacation in 1974, when I got married.

"At the time," he continues, "there was no specialization. A lawyer's practice included a wide variety of cases as well as a wide variety of clients. The Town of Richmond happened to be one of George Savoie's clients and, when I took over the practice, became one of mine. I pled quite a number of cases for the Town; a typical case could involve a sewage back-up problem, or a fracture suffered on an icy sidewalk. I was also asked quite frequently for my advice on a number of issues and problems facing the Town."

Because insurance costs were so high, the Town was under-insured. Hiring a lawyer to reach reasonable settlements for damages caused by broken water mains or potholes didn't strain the

Town's budget as much as insurance premiums. It was an expedient way of saving money. For the most part, the plan seemed to work. Then, in 1984, a fire broke out at the Town's water pumping station and the cost of being underinsured skyrocketed.

The fire also turned out to be the spark that ignited Martel's political career. "I'd been advising the Town on legal matters for over a decade, ever since I'd been practicing law. I lived in Richmond. I was involved in the community; for example, I'd been president of the Richmond Chamber of Commerce. But in particular, I was concerned by the Town's disinterest in promoting industry. I thought that was a mistake. André Lupien, who'd been mayor for over a decade, was retiring. I decided to throw my hat in the ring."

The fact that Martel was returned as mayor by acclamation in more than half a dozen elections speaks volumes. There have been issues over that time that brought his popularity into question, but certainly never his competence. For example, what is now the site of an architecturally challenged grocery store and its large parking lot was once a spacious park with a small fountain and children's playground. The mayor was widely criticized, both for sacrificing the green space and for permitting such a warehouse-style structure to be erected in the middle of town. Still, even those unhappy with one or another of his decisions continued to trust his competence as mayor.

During his time in office, he acted on his goal of promoting industrial development. Five or six years before he was elected, the Town had created the Comité de promotion industrielle de Richmond (CPIR) that had the mandate to attract businesses and industries to the area. Similar organizations had been created before, going back at least to the 1930s. In 2001, the American-owned Brown Shoe Company closed its Richmond factory, putting several hundred people out of work.

"It was a hard blow for the Town," Marc-André says, "and we responded by investing heavily in the CPIR. The position of commissar in charge had been a part-time position and we made it a full-time post, hiring Martin Lafleur to fill it. He's been both industrious and imaginative in drawing small and medium-sized businesses to our industrial park that has been enlarged twice to accommodate new shops and factories. We continue to invest in the CPIR; in recent years, the Town has committed some sixty-five thousand dollars annually to industry. "

Arguably, the crown jewels of the industrial park are two immense warehouses known as the *gare inter-modale* where merchandise can quickly and efficiently be moved from tractor trailers to rail cars and vice versa. The St. Lawrence & Atlantic Railway runs through Richmond but so too do Highways 55, 116, 143 and 243 so that, despite its small size, Richmond continues to be something of a major hub with goods coming and going east, south, and west, according to need.

After MRCs (or RCMs in English: Regional County Municipalities) started being created in 1981 to replace the county system, Martel succeeded in having the MRC office established in Richmond.

He was instrumental in the revitalization of Gouin Park, a one hundred-acre tract of land left to the Town by Blanche Gouin after her death in 1952 and now a very inviting and well-tended urban forest with several kilometres of meandering trails. He similarly contributed to the creation of Richmond's Parc nautique that offers kayak rides on the St. Francis, thereby making the river accessible to citizens and tourists alike.

Martel's legacy will also include the continued preservation of four notable buildings that have been given patrimonial status under his auspices: the former St. Paul's Church on Belmont Street that now houses the Centre de l'interprétation de l'ardoise, St. Bibiane's Church, its rectory, and the adjoining

Couvent Mont St-Patrice, all of which date to the late nineteenth century.

Not all successes and accomplishments are easily visible. It could be argued that Martel's single biggest contribution to Richmond was what he managed to accomplish in the way of reducing the Town's debt.

"When I was elected, in 1986," he says, "more than a third of the Town's budget went towards paying interest and capital on loans that had been taken out over the years. Richmond received a lot of help from the provincial government towards paying off those loans; today, less than two percent of the budget is spent on financing our debt."

As Martel steps away from the post he has held for three decades, he can look back and see how his Town has changed, and point to changes in which he had a hand. But what does he see when he looks ahead?

"Something has to happen," he says after a moment's reflection, "otherwise Richmond is going to continue its long decline. Richmond needs more people to develop the downtown area. Unfortunately, in my opinion, we lost an opportunity when we failed to convince the population to fuse with Cleveland."

An attempt in 1999 to fuse Richmond with the Village of Melbourne, the Township of Melbourne and the Township of Cleveland was only partially successful. The Village of Melbourne accepted to amalgamate with Richmond, but the rural townships of Melbourne and Cleveland voted against the idea.

Ironically, in 2000, when the provincial government began its program of forced amalgamations right across Quebec, the Richmond area seemed to go totally ignored.

"Richmond would have benefited from a merger," he continues. "We need more territory. We already have installations— our new well of potable water and our sewage treatment ponds in particular—that are situated in Cleveland.

"As well, towns and municipalities are controlled by the MRC and by the provincial government, and that makes our situation that much more complex. Our decision-making powers are often curtailed and restricted by the dictates of the MRC or of Quebec City.

"Still," he finishes, "there is room to be optimistic about Richmond's future. As long as we can continue to offer the quality of life, and in particular access to culture and recreation, that we enjoy today, we should continue to have people moving here to live and raise their families. When all is said and done, Richmond is a great place to live."

# Acknowledgements

I AM INDEBTED to a great many people who contributed to the making of this book, perhaps first and foremost to those who shared their stories. These include in no particular order, Jacques Marin, Sharon and Kurt, Michelle Nadeau, Erika Lockwood, Julie O'Donnell, Manon Morin, Danièle Normandin, Gisèle Leclerc, Réjeanne Roux, Anne-Marie Charland, Elizabeth Dupont, Donald Healy, Jérôme Desmarais, Jean-Roch Lapointe, Ron Booth, Billy Trippear, Kent Trippear, Donna and Sidney Mills, Micky Blemings, Jean-Roch Lapointe, Jacques Thibeault, Raymond Fortier, Anita Demers, Gilles Parent, Richard Arsenault, Marc-André Martel, Rémi-Mario Mayette, and Martin Lafleur.

Help in other forms came from Ali Ayachi and Julie Poulin. I also want to thank Karine Savary, archivist at the Société d'histoire de Sherbrooke and her staff, as well as the Société d'histoire de Drummondville, the Société généalogique de Drummondville and the Paroisse Ste-Bibiane.

I am particularly grateful to Esther Healy, archivist at the Richmond County Historical Society, who provided both material and photos for this book and invaluable direction when it was being drafted.

I owe a debt of gratitude to my publisher, Robin Philpot. Many thanks go to Barbara Rudnicka, Mireille Chamberland

and Karine Fonda for their attentive reading and thoughtful editorial advice.

Most of all, I want to thank Francine who, among many other things, is one of my most discerning readers.

# Further Reading

Booth, J. D. *Railways of Southern Quebec. Volume 2.* Toronto. Railfare, 1985.

Cleveland, Edward. *A Sketch of the early settlement and history of Shipton, Canada East.* Richmond, Quebec: 1858.

Coburn, Evelyn Lloyd, *F.S. Coburn, Beyond the Landscape.* Erin, Ontario: Boston Mills Press, 1996.

Day, Catherine. *History of the Eastern Townships,* Montreal, 1869.

Fonda, Nick. *Roads to Richmond, Portraits of Quebec's Eastern Townships.* Montreal, Quebec: Baraka Books, 2010.

Fonda, Nick. *Hanging Fred and a Few Others, Painters of the Eastern Townships.* Montreal, Quebec: Baraka Books, 2014.

Foxcurran, Robert, Bouchard, Michel, Malette, Sébastien. *Songs Upon the River.* Montreal, Quebec: Baraka Books, 2016.

Moreau, Guy. *Histoire de Windsor.* Windsor, 1997.

Richmond County Historical Society. *Annals of Richmond County and Vicinity, Vol. 1 & 2.* Richmond, Quebec, 1966, 1968.

St-Amant, Joseph-Charles. *Un coin des Cantons de l'Est : Histoire de l'envahissement pacifique mais irrésistible d'une race.* Drummondville, 1932

Saint-Pierre, Diane, Southam, Peter, Kesteman, Jean-Pierre. *Histoire des Cantons de l'est,* Institut québécois de recherche sur la culture, 1998.

Southam, Peter. *Irish Settlement and National Identity in the Lower St. Francis Valley.* Richmond, Quebec: The St. Patrick's Society of Richmond & Vicinity, 2012

Wilhelmy, Jean-Pierre. *Soldiers for Sale, German "Mercenaries" with the British in Canada During the American Revolution.* Montreal: Baraka Books, 2012.

Printed in September 2017
by Gauvin Press,
Gatineau Québec